Rappelling the Mennonite Mountain

RAPPELLING the MENNONITE MOUNTAIN

GOOD KID IN BAD OVERALLS

John E. Hildebrand

Epic Press

Belleville, Ontario, Canada

Library and Archives Canada Cataloguing in Publication

Hildebrand, John E., 1936-
    Rappelling the Menonite mountain / John E. Hildebrand.

ISBN 1-55306-890-4.--ISBN 1-55306-892-0 (LSI ed.)

1. Hildebrand, John E., 1936- --Childhood and youth. 2. Farm life--Manitoba--History--20th century. 3. Mennonites--Manitoba Biography.

I. Title.

BX8143.H55A3 2005   289.7'71'092   C2005-900235-2

To order additional copies, please contact:

John E. Hildebrand
#353
P.O. Box 8000
Abbotsford, BC V2S 6H1

Epic Press is an imprint of *Essence Publishing,* a Christian Book Publisher dedicated to furthering the work of Christ through the written word.. For more information, contact:
    20 Hanna Court, Belleville, Ontario, Canada K8P 5J2
    Phone: 1-800-238-6376 • Fax: (613) 962-3055
    E-mail: publishing@essencegroup.com
    Internet: www.essencegroup.com

Dedication

To my parents William and Elizabeth Hildebrand
who raised and taught me the values of the day.

To Susan's parents George & Elizabeth Schroeder
who raised and gave me a wonderful wife of forty-seven years
and counting.

Acknowledgements

What a privilege it is to devote a page to those that made this book possible, to publicly print the wonderful word, *thank you!*

The number of persons I have to recognize on this page is likely a record for brevity.

My first chapter was given to a retired English teacher who returned the scripted pages with more red ink comments I feel may well be another record. His large, printed letters, circled, asked the question every student dreads—"who was your English teacher or did you miss this class?"

Although encouraging—if the above comments are taken positively—locating another person to steer me right would be appreciated.

My many coffees with Abe Olfert, another retiree, from the printing trade, did keep the scattered ambers in my literary effort on at least life support.

Sure I had the correct person in mind from day one! My hang up about this choice was that she was 2,000 kilometres away, and I felt I would require "hands-on" help to bring this amber into a flame. Wrong!

Weeks of thought, possibly delay tactics, I made the request of her to be my editor, although I used less demanding words, not to scare her off.

The request was about as nerve-racking as was asking her older sister—some forty years ago—to marry me! At least this request was not on bent knee; well mentally it was close.

I listened to the "I am not qualified" stories, grunted just to keep the conversation alive, without a "no" of course.

Laura Skeavington, my sister-in-law, lives in Manitoba. A retired nurse she is, a compassionate person, yet over the years I had come to know that if I was making some edgy statements, Laura did not shy from lowering the boom on me! She has a "good nose"—despite her denials—in the literary world!

This was the person I required! Little did I know at the time how much I needed her critique at every level!

Before accepting the challenge, some weeks later, the second dreaded question, "Have you a job description?" I knew that to keep Laura on side the answer had to be *yes*, since she had made it abundantly clear that it would take many more people besides her to bring this book to fruition. I recall spewing a few names that thankfully came to me under the pressure I was under, assuring her that more persons were yet to be contacted that would round out the team. I knew Laura was detecting my attempt to give this line the look of a managed project. She was, however, hooked on the idea and not my charm allowed her to say "Lets go to work!"

Her job description was, err, a tad open at this time, adding that she would find a fit into these pages as we proceeded. Again the promises as vague as to her sister, accepted many years ago, except the one question on the lifetime or unto death do us part, that one I answered with conviction and am still defining the perimeters, as permissions are granted me! The rest were about as open as the editorship was in this case.

My most "perfect stories," the ones I was sure were "print ready," were returned with fine red print in the columns, words were circled, question marks hanging like candy canes at Christmas!

My biggest problem was that I knew Laura was right, as always!

Laura was my favorite sister-in-law before, you are now even closer to me! The hundreds of hours she invested towards my dream book, perhaps thousands, what makes it such a privilege to acknowledge your work at the front of this book! Without your generosity of time and no doubt at times agonizing how to correct the sentence when it did not read right, the late nights you could not sleep, because thoughts "were gnawing at your brain."

The "E-mails of correction" I received from Laura were anticipated, yet also a measure of disquiet when I saw the amount of comments in the columns or lines, always in that menacing, red tone. The most troubling comments were when it read "unacceptable" with no further assistance as to the nature of the problem, not even a hint as to correcting the infraction. Laura knew how to push my buttons, and push them she did! Wonderful!

To Laura's husband of also near forty years, Don, a huge *thank you!* Many times that late cup of Java she inhaled over my manuscript, rather than the back rub you hoped for!

To my wife and children, your indifference to my literary efforts caused me to press on, determined that I could bring these thoughts of my youth between the covers of some varnished firm pages. Inspiration comes in many forms! Fruits and veggies—while good for us—do at times come in tart tastes!

To Essence Publishing, fellow Christians, your understanding was appreciated!

Table of Contents

Preface

*R*appelling *the Mennonite Mountain* is intended to focus on the growing up years, the boyhood, of a farm lad in southern Manitoba. Being "above the world" in morals, ethics and religion caused many an additional challenge to a Mennonite youngster, but did inspire the book title! Not a regular farm kid, if there is such a thing as "regular," but rather a Mennonite farm boy! "Everyone's youth is unique" is my approach to life. So many books that are written just gloss over the younger years of a person's life. These young years are the easiest going and carefree of the memories we create! All is fresh, new, just has to be tried or experienced. Innocence is a virtue. The world is your stage and beckoning to hear what you have in mind for it!

That I have wondered and marveled about "life," readers will become very aware. The fact that I have wandered some in my youth may be the reason for the "wondering part."

The book is intended for lighter reading, and its contents are likely to stimulate memories of your own childhood. If so, stop and ponder them. If the book succeeds in "you pondering," then you will no doubt be enriched to have relived memories relegated to the archives of your mind, you may have thought were non-retrievable, dare I suggest non-existent!

At times, as you read, it may appear that I was a rebellious youth. If you determine that I was, so be it!

In my mind, I feel I was not rebellious, but prepared to challenge a Mennonite system or heritage that was stuck in a rut and ought to be moved along with the changing world. Was I cognizant of the fact that I was "kicking some against the traces?" Hardly—but I was restless.

Striking a balance between life's hard facts and the humour that's mixed in was a concern. Sure fifty-fifty is a fair balance, no math professor could argue that. However what is humour to me, may be hard facts to you, or where does a pinch of melancholy come in—did I mean melodrama? How do you proportion the components of a "riot"? Maybe it was only a "dust up."

Yes, one could ask friends about one's youth, remembering in the nick of time that a camel is actually a racehorse, but designed by a committee! That nixes that idea!

After a fierce battle with myself—no, it was a debate—it was decided to best allow the reader to slice and dice the situations, the percentages between this and that!

The caveat "reader beware" its my "top" line! Remember as you read my yarn, its easier to tell a story when you are the only one telling it!

Growing up as a lad on a mixed farm is possibly one of the most exciting youth episodes that a human can experience, likely explains one of the reasons Mennonites choose farming as a livelihood and expressing honour to God!

In reading this tale, some may question the amount of space devoted to the act (art) of reproduction, be it with animals or the production of grains or the veggies in the garden. A farm, is reproduction! A successful farmer depends totally on each and every animal, grain, yes, even the human species to reproduce. Without reproduction, he is no longer a farmer! A large family, a huge barn never hurt no farmer! The bushels per acre the grains yield, the number of piglets a sow brings forth, the amount of potatoes his garden yields, will define the farmer's success or failure. The acts of reproduction in each grain, animal and human display God's sense of awe, yet humour. The blossoms on the fields or in the garden are spectacular! The reproduction act in animals can range from the unbelievable to the hilarious, remember ordained by God! A mixed farm over the years may have hundreds of varieties and species reproducing, for a lad to see and question! All precisely as God planned it for us, the hundreds, yea thousands, of years ago! Scientists love to add zeros to the ages to suit their theories or imagination!

Only man and woman did God give a Soul to, the ability to make choices between good and evil! How well we, as humans, have carried this responsibility, God will be the sole judge of.

For a lad to grow up, see the wonders, the excitement of the happenings on a mixed farm is mind boggling! From the descriptions given here, it is no secret that my fascination was boggled on a regular basis! No doubt this also stirred the wondering and wandering in my mind, even body!

God's sense of humour in the shape or size of each living creature he made, how they reproduced, making farmers successful defies description!

So in these anecdotes I have attempted to chronicle the fascination of a young lad growing up and each new day seeing another new process of God's plan unfolding before his eyes. That I was not always cognizant of the unfolding of "my universe" on a daily basis is often too routine to be fully appreciated at the time. Hindsight is the process where this facet of God's creation can best see the wonders and enjoy the marvelous recollections!

It is said that the further one can look back, seeing one's history, the further one can see into the future!

This book lends itself to be read slowly, stopping to re-capture your childhood, be it on the farm or in a hamlet or city.

Every geographical location on this planet provides a book of memories for each child!

Giving your memory time to retrieve these treasures that you may have thought were forgotten will return with pleasure and beauty of these recaptured thoughts, hopefully appreciated in a new way!

God has given us the gift of laughter, let's use it! Even some painful moments of the past, when recalled years later, do hold a laugh or two that should not go unspent! We don't stop laughing because we grow old, we grow old because we stop laughing!

Although not mentioned in each story, it is to be assumed that God is in each article, at least that is my basic assumption as I was chronicling these thoughts.

Just four words to my Rocky Mountain relatives, you were a blast!

Just where is Rocky Mountain in Southern Manitoba? It's not shown on the map as such, yes there are rocks, but no huge mountains— a few rolling hills, I concede. Did Robin Hood ever define the boundaries of Sherwood Forest? The mythical Rocky Mountain, should it receive the dignity of Capital letters?

Osterwick could be part of this imagination. Schanenfeld did have a gully. The one-five area, with the adjoining one-six area are also somewhat undefined. Glencross, Mason, I read that name on a pickle jar. Valleyfield, no, no that's in Quebec! La Raviere did have a ski jump at one time, that's too French for Rocky Mountain!

The memories I have chronicled here, plus the many still tucked away in far reaches of ones mind, I would want to do all over again! You were a slice! I trust you can laugh with me and, if required, at me! I know I have missed many nuggets.

You will find that I poke fun at my siblings, the fact that I was born fourth in the family of five. Should my siblings be writing their book, I feel certain that I would be the one getting poked at, it's all in good fun! Some names in the book have been changed to hopefully add a pinch of mystique and also some stories have, while basically true, been "dressed up" a bit for smoother reading. The older we get, the better we were, likely comes into play in my memories!

Adding new hues and colours to an old structure does wonders to the creations of yesteryear!

Happy memories,
The Author

Jugs and Jars

A few paces down the root cellar steps with my short legs of two years; a slip, tumble, a two gallon jug of vinegar smashed into many pieces, a deep gash cut to the top of the head, and my first recollections of life had begun!

The chug of a Model A Ford car caught my attention! Just celebrated my second birthday a few days before, and the excitement of knowing I was growing up made every moment one to be taken advantage of.

Traveling salesmen made their rounds on a regular basis to the farms in Flatfields. "Peddlers" was the code or common name for these men. Today we could make some comparisons with the Amway method of selling, but the names way back were Familex, Watkins, and Rawlies, as well as others.

Since housewives did not get into the town market place often (once a month would be often), there was a need for these services the peddlers offered at the farm house door. Needless to say, competition was keen between the various peddlers and visits to farms became too frequent and time consuming for the housewives.

Various ways of communicating this "not welcome or don't need anything" were discussed between farmhouse wives, ranging from simply not answering the door, to opening the door a crack and saying, "We are fine." Even a crack of the door was enough to start the peddler's verbal pitches, as he was accustomed to "getting the bums rush," and some peddlers became quite brazen; a foot in the door became a fact, not just a saying! Extreme stories got around about how peddlers were encouraged to leave and not return. When a peddler had been repeatedly asked to refrain from calling on this farm, the house wife lost her cool; when he knocked on the door again, she had the swill pail handy (pig feed scraps from kitchen leftovers with lots of liquids) and promptly dumped it on his head! It worked. At last sighting, the peddler had "chosen a new area" to ply his trade. The story of this lark spread far and wide with the peddlers business badly effected.

Then, too, there were other situations that provided a "bonus" for the amorous peddler. Mennonites seem to love telling the story, but it's always *"yanna zaad"* (the other person said). These cases were indeed rare, but the talk about the few actual cases that occurred was not rare, making for gossip at visitations on an otherwise drab landscape.

Some peddlers were modest in their efforts to sell, while others kept on showing, promoting products that would help the salesperson meet his quota, but Mom also had a budget to work with and that seemed to escape the peddler as much as it did me.

The vanillas, the drink powders all smelled so good, while the more practical items like soaps etc. were oft times overpriced, making Mom a tough sell.

Moms reputation for being a top cook in the area was known to those that frequented our home; the traveling peddlers were also well aware of Moms culinary skills, having taken in the aroma that emanated from the kitchen. So when the Model A car came chugging up the driveway this morning, Mom's mind had deeper thoughts than mine, as she glanced at the clock. It was 11:15 a.m. and not only were the peddlers aware of Mom's tasty meals, they also knew that to take part in such a meal, it meant being at our house early, otherwise it was a missed meal! The peddler would "work" the neighbourhood and time his calls so that eleven fifteen was the time to call at our home.

The peddlers were also, for the most part, quite willing to reward Mom with some free product in exchange for the meal. There were times when, well, we just did not need any products, the budget was tight or the peddler of the day did not have Mom's favorite products. Even worse, the salesperson was known to be too persistent for Mom once he got his foot in the door. The peddlers that had "a glint" in their eye were referred to (in whispers) as "tomcats," and at our house that meant "a no sale of anything!" The "not at home trick" or a good bye wave from the window, was called into play. Pup was unrestrained!

It was of course another idle farm trick to observe (and talk) which farmyard such a "tomcat" guy was giving the time of day. His arrival time and departing time seemed to cause giggles when Dad and Mom related the observations or they were relayed to them from other neighbours. In an otherwise boring neighbourhood, this was as close to excitement as you came many months.

One time when a peddler did call and Mom did not allow him in the door (our dog Pup was allowed to circle the car), the salesman left in somewhat of a huff. As he was leaving the yard, he ran over a hen free-ranging on our yard without even slowing down. The chicken was dead, with parents upset that the peddler did not make an effort to slow down and avoid hitting the precious egg layer. A few months later when the same salesman again came to the yard, Dad was at home and the chicken was still high on Dad's mind. Dad met the peddler before he got out of the vehicle, explained that we really did not wish him to call at our home anymore. The peddler denied even having felt a bump as he hit the hen. This peddler was one of the more persistent ones and the products he sold did not appeal to Mom, which made his banning from the yard almost a pleasure. The peddler left in a huff again, did not call till a year later, was reminded that the ban was still in effect, never to be seen again!

The peddler that called today did have some of Mom's favorite products, also rewarded her well with free products when the peddler asked to join us at the noon meal. Dad came in for dinner (dinner in Mennonite terms is served at noon, the 6 p.m. meal was referred to as supper), the meal was ready on the wood cook stove, so the word "offer" was somewhat redundant. Should Dad not be home for the noon meal, no peddler received a meal at our house.

While the meat, potatoes and veggies were cooking on the stove, on this occasion I believe it was home made perogies with home-cured ham, while the coffee kettle was whistling on the hot stove. As the coffee was heating, the peddler was busy showing the suitcase of goodies he had. His case was always jammed, make closing it an art or miracle. The "suitcase," or business attache, reminded me of a completed picture puzzle, every piece had the correct spot and each product, when shown, had to be replaced at the exact spot in order to be able to close his display case. After the peddler's mild presentation had been made, Mom had made some choices, the peddler would leave for the car to get the items that received a yes. The open display case and the discussion between the folks, plus my ignored wishes about an extra product or two, was too no avail. Many times however, when the peddler returned from getting items from the car and bringing them to our house, additional items were needed and the extra sale had been made. The open product case had worked its magic.

The exciting part for me was when the products Mom wanted had been agreed upon and the cash transaction was about to take place. The peddler reached in his deep, oversized pant pockets, judging by the fact that his arm disappeared nearly to his elbow to reach that wallet at the bottom of his pocket.

The wallet, once extricated from his pocket, was actually like a leather bag, the best description is seeing a huge bull from the backside. His ample appendage and the peddler's purse were very close in appearance! In fact that style of purse was called in Low German, "*ein beadle,*" which strangely enough is precisely what a bull's appendage is called! The purse was rather like a large softball when closed but when he held the top metal snap closure and allowed gravity to set in, it was a *thud-thud*, sometimes another *roll-thud* sound, and the purse was now about a foot long! In it some compartments held some bills, but it seemed pretty much "a dig" to find the correct change required. This wallet held endless fascination for me! Like, how much money is in there? Does he empty it every night? Where does he buy a wallet like that?

On this particular day, the business part had been done first and the aroma from the kitchen told us that the meal was nearly ready to enjoy. Mom wanted to go into the basement, which was really a root cellar. The unique part was that the cellar door was part of the living room floor. It was a lid (trap door) three feet wide by five feet long and opened length wise, leaning against the wall when open. The cellar held all the potatoes, onions, beets, even watermelons, plus all of Mom's preserves, jams and jellies, which all combined would be about 200 jars. Mom had laboured many long hours during the hot summer to prepare these sealed delicacies, most of it before harvest but some after as well, to be sure her family and guests would be well looked after throughout the winter and next spring.

So on this day, when the peddler and Dad are chatting, Mom decides that a jar of that special preserve would just round the meal off nicely. She opened the cellar lid, assuming that my little mind would remain engrossed in the men's conversation, she proceeded down the rather steep steps into the eight-feet-deep cellar. Without a sound, I decided that Mom would surely require my input as to which preserve to pick, and I followed Mom down the steep steps. She had reached the bottom, while I took my first steps at the top. My short, two-year-old legs were no match for the adult, wooden "glorified ladder" steps, down I went, ass over tea kettle!

At the bottom of the stairs sat a two gallon glass jug of vinegar, which my head aimed for, struck my target perfectly, broke the jug wide open into many jagged edges, which promptly cut a deep gash on the top of my ample head. With blood gushing, plus my screams, Dad came running and carried me up the stairs in his strong arms, laying me on the wooden sleeper bench. A sleeper bench (*schlup banck*) was a homemade affair, but by a craftsman of the day. About six feet long and three feet wide, it was used for sitting (or snoozing on) during the day but at night when the 'sitting lid" was opened, the front pulled out, it slept two or more youngsters. It was a 1930s style futon bed. Between Dad, Mom and the peddler they shaved the hair on top of my head, then washing my hair to be sure none remained inside the gash. The peddler had an antiseptic wash that was also placed around the wound. They then pinched the gash shut with their fingers, reducing the blood flow.

The sales rep, having just the right cure in his suitcase, promptly applied a few aspirins and my sobs died down, while at the same time hearing a lecture of sorts from frustrated parents!

The meal was delayed for the adults and I missed one of the few meals in my life! The aspirins made me sleepy. When I

24

woke up, I found a quarter the peddler had left on the bench beside me.

The top of my head was tender for a very long time, no doctor became involved. As the saying goes, the difference between a good and a bad haircut is about ten days. I was back in vogue in no time at all, with a somewhat curbed curiosity for a while.

The peddler, practicing his public relations, always inquired about my wound on future visits, having a spare quarter in that long wallet of his for me. He always commented on my bravery, which was a welcome switch from hearing about my stupidity from the family!

Brightly shines the sun—and the Son!

Sleepless in Spears

Being a very active lad all my youth, I would "adventure till I dropped" every day and night!

My mom rather often—and not at a time of my choosing—would remind me that I had been a handful as a baby, with the closing portion of the saga a common refrain "and you are a handful today!"

My days inside the family cradle do sound exciting as described by Mom and siblings! It was all of four feet long, rather deep, with the rounded runners below cut from two-inch thick wood, the sides being of equal thickness.

From later years when my younger brother claimed residency in this heavy duty contraption, I recall it so well and any chance of me forgetting a minor detail were eliminated by the repeated stories of my nights in this box of horrors! Regretfully I admit I cannot recollect even a tiny particle of this experience, which saddens me! Here I had a chance to "be the fly on the wall" of the folk's bedroom and what do I do? I sleep through most of it and remember none of activities there!

You could have rocked an elephant in this bombproof shelter, I thought but was relieved that thought did not occur to my precious Mom as she regaled the story to each set of visitors. It seems, according to Mom telling guests, that I was a real tough guy to get to fall asleep. To aid this sleeping process, Dad would place a piece of broom handle where the runner would be compelled to rock across, giving it that sleepy bounce. That, she carried on, with a quick look around at the guests, was for the "other kids." Providing I was dumb enough to hang around or she had clamped an arm over my shoulder, the feature story continued, with Mom's pointy finger clearly in my direction or pressed in my neck, had I not used evasive tactics well before the story reached this stage. *"Fa Hauns brooked wie an knabel holt unya di vage!"* (For Johnny we used a piece of cord lumber under the runner). This huge bounce then helped close my eyes. If the visitors still indicated that they were titillated by these yarns, Mom could add on different versions of how they had stopped rocking too soon, thinking I was asleep but was not and bellowed before the rocking process was restarted. There was about a two-year break between each of the first four kids but the fifth had a near seven-year postponement after me.

Mercifully, Mom spared those delayed details from me and the guests but I can only assume that my untimely waking up in the evening ruined many an amorous moment, likely causing the lack of my younger brother being born for some years! My ungrateful younger brother has never thanked me for him being many years younger than he was intended to be, perhaps!

Whenever a car ride at night was involved in our family social life, it was a given that I would be fast asleep after two turns of the Model A Ford's narrow but tall wheels. The clay pothole roads simulated the cradle's thump well, in fact too well as my story tells.

In the back seat, likely between a mix of sisters or brother—at times all three—the scenery and acoustics were not a factor—not when your eyes are closed! The top speed of twenty-five miles per hour of the rattletrap car took an hour from the Rocky Mountain area where the relatives lived to our home on the Flatlands.

According to (unreliable) reports I "did grouse a bit" when they attempted to wake me upon finally arriving home from our adventure with the Rocky Mountain hill-billy relatives. Threats to the effect that the folks might just let me sleep in the car the rest of the night did not faze me. In fact, next morning I was unaware that I supposedly had grumped when they woke me for the trek from car to my little bed. Just three years old, I slept just off Mom and Dad's bedroom—which was the living room to be exact—in a makeshift but comfy bed.

Another trip to Rocky Mountain, yet another active night of adventure with my cousins. The trip home was a replica of the past—fast asleep in a shake, rattle and bump. It was a beautiful warm night, with the sky loaded with stars, at least that was the rumour later. When we arrived at home, the normal fuss when they attempted to wake me. Mom and Dad agreed, apparently, no doubt with the strong encouragement of the frustrated siblings, "Let him sleep in the car."

It was a nice warm summer night and I slept in the model A while the rest of the family went to their respective bedrooms. I certainly hope I stretched out on that back seat for maximum comfort!

In the morning it was customary for me to sleep in. The family had their breakfast, sisters and brother off to school, with the parents completing the farm chores. Everyone forgot about me sleeping in the car!

I did awake—ah yes—they had made good on their threat to allow me to sleep in the car which was parked in the large car garage—tool shed, as well as granary. At this point my bravado was intact!

I sleepily got out of the model A Ford car, attempting to leave the garage, heading for the house and a big breaky that I felt I surely deserved. A small delay was that I found the heavy door latch was too high for me to reach. A handy wooden apple box should fix that. Stepping onto the box, I could reach the latch all right but it was a tight fit door latch and I could not nudge it.

Now some panic did set in. I called for my collie Pup. Yes he came but through the large front window of the garage I saw his wagging tail and drooling tongue. Pup did go for help but my busy Dad did not interpret Pup's uneasiness and his running to the garage and back! One can only imagine the frustration Pup must have gone through with not being able to convey the emergency message to a daft Father that his young protege was indeed in some difficulty!

Some big tears now ran down my chubby cheeks. Yes I said—blow the car horn—which will surely remind the parents where I am locked in. The Model A horn pleaded—aaaauuuu-uwahwah, but only Pup was excited as I peered out the garage window. Repeat blowing of the car's horn brought some results but not immediate nor what I had hoped for.

Now I see Dad—through some misty eyes! But while Pup is bouncing around outside the garage door, my dad scurries to our elderly Bergen's yard next door neighbours, to see if he can be of help, having heard the car horn sounding.

The flow of tears increased. Shouting to Dad as I did—he walked to the neighbours—Dad did not hear me and ignored the fussing collie. Pup did not even make an attempt to follow Dad, as he was generally want to do.

When the neighbours said they were fine but had also heard the car horn—curiously coming from our yard. Then Dad's light bulb went on bright! I knew Dad was fast, but when he came bounding towards the car garage, his feet appeared to be wasting time touching the ground! Pup was just ahead of him, as the collie had seen Dad scurrying back and went to meet him part way and was now leading the fray towards our garage and my cries! Pup knew he now had Dad's attention and was determined to be part of the rescue mission—he was!

The garage door flung open and a very shaken lad was safe in his Father's arms! As to who shed more tears, I can not say!

Coming into the house was a tear-stained Dad and son, while Mom turned deathly white! In panic she ran into the living room were I was assumed to be sleeping. She returned in audible, disbelieving tears!

Mom snatched me from Dad's strong arms, while our hugs & tears mingled!

Pup was whining outside the screen door to remind us that he too was hurting, his tail on a slow wave, and also reminding that he really had been the first to answer my call—perhaps feeling a pat on his golden mane would not be to much to ask.

Soon I was outside playing but Mom & Dad remained in the house for a considerable time. Never again was the subject discussed in our house! Never another mention of allowing me to sleep in the car—even when I was ornery about walking to the house from the car, after those sleepy trips!

While this event when spelled out in black and white, may sound cruel or at least crass—I feel it was neither! Hill-Billy bad judgement, well yes, there was a measure of that. The intent of the parents was genuine. Certainly, they had reasoned, they would fetch me first thing in the morning from the car before I even woke up.

It was a case of simply an oversite on every family member's part. Mom and Dad were both feeling terrible, with the subject never again discussed—nor repeated, at least in my presence. In fact, when at a family gathering some three decades later, a reminiscing session broke out. Many interesting stories being regaled, most I felt had now received a "few coats of varnish" to make them a tad more refined, since times had changed the dull past needed a brightening up. I had the audacity to tell "my sleeping in the model A story." A hush fell over folks and siblings! As though I had cut off their oxygen, none could recall this event, yeah, not only that, not as much as a single question about the event was asked, while uncomfortable eyes searched the floor to change the subject! This was clearly one of those no-no stories that likely most families have. The ones that you would prefer to rewrite history if one could. As the main player in the story, I happen to think it was funny and bears repeating.

A few tears were shed—make that quite a few—a scare for a youngster—but all was repaired in minutes!

Dad somewhat sheepishly did return to the neighbours to report that all was well.

I had had a good night's sleep, a nice breakfast —I was allowed extra cream on my puff wheat that morning—with a busy day after that! The hand full of cookies was not mentioned as I left the house.

Pup settled for the "one for you, one for me" arrangement of the cookie deal as per norm. I did however allow him the last two cookies, a smack of the tongue, a big fluffy tail wave, that long collie snout staring those beady eyes into mine, with that "What did you have in mind for today?" look!

Threshing Days

The summer had been good to me. Yes, there had been times when, even as a four-year-old, I had felt "just a bit rushed," but that was now behind me! Helping gathering eggs, pulling weeds in the garden, hauling the same fresh luscious green weeds to the pigpens with my new red wooden "flyer" wagon can interfere with a young man's tight schedule! Those beady pig eyes and long dirty snout are forever hungry, it seems.

But that was a vague memory for the moment, and uppermost in my mind was the threshing season! Yes, I did recall enough of the last year's threshing season that made me really determined that this year, an entire twenty-five percent older than last year, I would not only observe this operation, I would be a part of it!

It was mid August and the crops were early this year, I had overheard Dad and the other men talking. The past few weeks had been really hot and thus I had my large straw hat on my "rather large head which was connected to my stocky body," via a short neck. Comments were made by uncles that I was a "*klutz.*" In those days, in Low German, that was referring to a hefty sized wooden block that every farmyard had one or two of in the repair shop. In English it was a "block" and on this block, ours was three feet in diameter and about thirty inches high, many farm repairs were performed. But it was standard fare to have a young stocky guy referred to as a "klutz," especially since I was the only one in the family that was "well built!" My siblings and parents looked a tad undernourished, which was far from the case, I just happened to carry my food well! So while the summer had been good, the best was yet to come: threshing season!

Dad had, for several weeks now, left early in the morning with his prize team of jet black Clydesdale horses, Jack and Frank they had been named, and came into our farmyard as colts, bought from an Uncle.

They were now gentle, peace-loving giants, and my parents had little concern when I roamed freely with them in the barn or the pasture. A carrot or a handful of oats snuck from Dad's grain bins always had Jack and Frank coming to me. Yes, we had a number of other horses but these two would be at my side first and any attempt at intruding this inner circle by other horses was quickly dealt with by "my Jack and Frank"!

Yes Dad was away threshing as part of the threshing gang, the gang that I was waiting to come to our farm. A threshing gang could be various sizes: about eight or ten team of horses, hayracks, a few field pitchers, a threshing machine with large tractor to drive the unit.

I remembered those broad shouldered men from last year's threshing bee. The large hats to keep the sun away from their eyes and keep the head a bit cooler, short sleeved shirts with the bulging biceps showing, that I so looked forward to having on my arms! Tough looking ankle high leather shoes, that seemed "well worn" day after new. The tough hands when they squeezed my shoulder. To me, they were all friends—giants they were, but, in my mind, who could resist the smile of "a grown-up grin from a four year old" and not think of me as an equal! They were all "dads" to someone was my premise, as a result they had no choice but to like me!

The summer air had changed, so I had heard it said. Ah yes, now I could also tell, fall was setting in. The many farm trees were beginning to lose the green and some hints of orange and gold were evident. While that fact was troublesome to some adults, that winter was nigh, not to me at this time. Would have time to worry about that, if required, in order to be seen as adult, later. For now, threshing totally permeated my entire being!

The smell of freshly threshed straw was in the soft warm breeze. Yes, the threshing action was a mile away, but the aroma of the freshly threshed straw carried well. That huge straw blower was tossing the straw and chaff fifty or more feet into the air, and the breeze was used as wings to transport the aroma over the now dehydrated countryside.

A threshing gang was formed to take care of the labour problem every farmer faced at this time of year. Tilling the soil, planting the seeds, that a farmer could handle with his family but threshing was not that way, it was hugely labour intensive and costly equipment. Huge pieces of equipment were required that no one farmer could afford and use only six weeks a year, sit idle the other weeks. The labour was similar, eight teams of horses with racks, the men to stook the sheaves onto the racks and haul them to the thresher. A semi-retired farmer, whose son was now manning the family farm, formed a threshing gang. The gang master, as he was known, would than assemble ten farmers around him—as many as fifteen in rare cases. These farmers would now work at each other's farms as the threshing progressed. The farmer's reward was that his farm's crop got threshed, and the gang master was paid by the bushel of grain threshed. No other cash changed hands.

Cash flow on the farm, for the most part, was the cream from the cows and eggs the chickens laid. These products were bartered for groceries (that the farm did not provide), shoes and clothing.

Grain was fed to the farm animals, however excess grain was hauled to the local elevators and produced the cash to pay the bank for the farm loan. The banker in these farm towns knew that the best time of year the loan payments to the bank would be made was "after the harvest." The bankers had heard all the hard luck stories before; most, like my dad, took a loan very seriously, and if a delay in harvesting occurred he would go see the banker with his facts, setting a new date for the payment to be made. Not all farmers did so, and the banker was amazed that some farmers were still "threshing at Christmas time," at least, according to the "non-payment" of the overdue loan!

The joining of forces to harvest the crop solved the labour and huge investment in equipment problem, every one was happy, well most times. The gang master was the one that decided whose farm would be threshed next. The first consideration was that a farmer's entire crop, be it wheat, oats, barley flax, all be ready for threshing once the threshing outfit made its way onto the farm. This saved travel and set up time for the gang master and precious sunshine hours. Not all the farmers were happy with the gang master's decisions. The gang master had that human side to him, and a brother in the gang, perhaps a long serving gang member like my dad, did get the nod ahead of others at times. The gang master loved my mom's cooking and times, when he was hungry, perhaps he listened to his stomach and overrode other logic, with our farm threshed next! Most times it amounted to grumbling from the waiting farmers but seldom was the gang master challenged.

My dad was small in stature but his work ethics were tall; the gang master was well aware of this. Dad was at work first in the morning and last to leave the thresher at night. While he had a huge sense of humour, work was work, with humour mixed into the day. Many times when the sun was beginning to set on the flat prairie, Mom would be wondering when Dad might be expected home from his days threshing at other farms. Mom always had a good hot meal for him when he arrived home. To help answer her question, I would walk about a half mile or so, with my trusty collie dog called Pup.

Pup was there when I arrived in the world and my parents, being basic in life, came up with the name "Pup" for our collie. I would have liked to call him "Hero" or "Beethoven," "Lassie" would have been more accurate but Pup was too well-established for me to tinker with his name, and Pup he remained!

So down the road I could see the thresher spewing straw from the blower on the neighbour's field. When Dad fed the thresher from his last rack of the day (dew was settling in), I could tell it was Dad's rack at the thresher by the amount of straw being blown out of that straw tube. With a well-fed thresher, the straw blower reflected this action! I then reported this revelation to my mom, who would prepare the hot meal and Dad was so surprised that her timing was so close when he arrived home. Although never said, I think Dad knew the trick we had and on his last load likely became superman in his pitching of sheaves. Knowing that by doing so, he was sending a clear signal to his messenger son and more importantly Mom, a hard long day stooking sheaves does make a guy hungry. More so, if you were threshing at a farm where the hostess was not that good at estimating the amount of food required to feed a threshing gang. Allowing that Dad's taste buds had been spoilt by Mom's culinary delights, and the host farmer's wife was accustomed to making "gut filler"!

As a young lad, I was amazed at how many neighbours or the gang master in the "off-harvesting season" just happened to drop by our yard about 11:20 a.m. for a quick word with Dad. The dinner invite always came and that "quick drop-in and a few words" with Dad, somehow became a goodbye at 1:15 p.m., after very appropriate compliments had been paid to Mom for the always scrumptious meal served.

My mom, while not "superstitious" (not a Mennonite, goodness), she did have more than her fair share "of hunches"! Whenever she just happened to bake a pie or fresh buns, sure enough, someone did show up to partake in the goodies, it could be the hunch she got when she dropped that kitchen knife on the floor. The knife pointed in a certain direction and if the opportunistic visitor came from the direction the knife had pointed to, that justified the baking and translated into all sorts of future hunches and goodies baked. Dropping the dish cloth on Saturday morning caused a flurry of mixing, stirring and baking the rest of the day, because visitors were definitely coming on Sunday! The strange problem was, Mom was right so often and the rare times she was wrong, the feast that our family had on late Sunday, carrying into Monday, sometimes Tuesday, we made Mom feel so good about being wrong!

Whenever Dad was working at a "certain farm" and she knew the hostess there was a "stingy food maker" for the gang, she would pack a sandwich or two for Dad to put under the hayrack, in that secret toolbox. Mom also knew that Dad, having a soft spot for others, would share at least one sandwich with a hungry gang member who was far away from home and was at the mercy of the meager offerings of the hostess. The cookies she had also packed were well received and can't recall any food ever coming back with Dad untouched! The gang master would have a talk with the host farmer when the grumbling became a bit much, who then was to discuss the delicate matter of "quantity" of food with his wife. The quantity could be ramped up some but the quality—cold potatoes, tasteless gravy, either eggs cooked green or totally under done, etc.—that remained status quo! Complaints or comments to the gang master after the one talking to the farmer, were met with "let's get on to the next farm before lunch tomorrow"!

A hayrack consisted of four steel wheels, two feet tall, a nine by fourteen feet wooden flat deck, with an eight-feet-high rack at each end. Angle side braces kept the load intact. The horses had a ten feet oak pole, called a tongue, running between them. The tongue allowed the horses to steer the rack, as well as back it up. The "tongue concept" was the basis for most farm horse drawn wagons and implements.

Having the hayrack harnesses and horses in good condition, well trained, was important to the gang master. Breakdowns meant the rack rotation would be altered, which the gang master noted, and likely a breakdown meant the threshing machine, having to wait for sheaves. The gang master had little patience for such delays, and a talking-to was assured! On rare occasions, a parting of the ways if the farmer did not accept the gang master's rebuke and spoke back in disrespect. The gang master, had to be fair but very firm to retain the respect of the rest of his award winning threshing members.

Also, the skills of the farmers horses and driver were noted. Handling skills of the horse team at the thresher was required at times, out of the normal and this, when handled well, was noted by all, including the hostess wife and perhaps daughter who just happened to observe this from a distance or a chance visit to the thresher. (There were, after all, a few single men in the gang!) At the loaded dinner table, when the host wife or daughter did, rather loudly, compliment the driver involved in the special feat they had witnessed, the other drivers became quieter, while the complimented driver seemed to sit up rather tall! After the dinner feast was over and the men filed out the kitchen, burping, yet regretfully leaving, the complimented driver would give

Mom a wink or pinch in the ribs (sometimes both). Mom seemed to be getting caught close to the exit, quite frequently. Everyone enjoys a compliment and this was Mom's turn to shine!

Even in the fields, the horse's behaviour was noted and reported by other drivers, if poor habits became the norm for a few team drivers. By strange coincidence, the farms where "meagre offerings" were given to the men, the same farmers horses were often the ones complained about to the gang master. Poorly fed horses before coming to work, meant the animals could not resist grabbing a few bites from the host farmer's oat stocks and spoiling the sheaves as they pulled the rack. Farmers had little tolerance for such waste. It was noted on his own farm this poor horse feeder guy would place mesh baskets over the horses nose and mouth, so the horses could not take a nip.

At other farms, he condoned such nipping of sheaves from the horses! Either the guilty farmer accepted the admonishment of the gang master, corrected his ways by feeding his horses properly, or risked not being invited back to the threshing gang next year! This gang master had a waiting list of farmers hoping to become a part of this crack group! The horses, when well trained, would pull the rack as it was being loaded from the long row of stocks on the field just at the right pace and even stop without command when the farmer got behind on the loading. A well-trained team was prized by the owner and well cared for. They were spoken to in near-affectionate terms and received many a pat on the neck when the farmer walked by. Horses, like dogs, respond to compliments with even greater efforts! Since Dad had a well-trained team of horses and knew how to handle them well, was at the receiving end of many host wives compliments as they had noted his prowess at handling his team. These compliments and the resulting winks were documented at home by a proud Dad while Mom was patient, she knew she to could "hold her own" with some good-natured flirting when the gang was at our farm and she did! This added to the threshing festive mood for all concerned, always a harmless activity. Mom's culinary selections were "five star dinner" raves, thus translated into winks and hugs. Mom always wore a freshly starched apron and her hair was in place, making the paying of a compliment even easier!

After weeks, but it seemed like an eternity, Dad came home and finally uttered those long awaited words, "Tomorrow, late afternoon, we should be finished threshing at the other farm and the 'outfit' [as the threshing unit was oft referred to] shall be coming to our farm!" Pure music to my tender ears! Mom however was more reserved, "When will the men require a meal?" "A later lunch will be fine," Dad assured her. Mom looked a bit relieved. A "lighter lunch" to Mom of course would qualify as a full meal on many other farms, and knowing which farm the gang was coming from, the men would be hungry! Her menu had been well planned and it was a matter of choosing a menu page most suitable. Dad also added that a downturn in weather might be happening, according to the gang-masters arthritic knee. "Might not be threshing much before the weather takes over, hopefully not a long delay" had been the statement to Dad.

On red alert, that's the best way to describe my next morning! Dad was long gone by the time my "sun rose." Had a quick breakfast and was out the door before Mom could think of something "small" that I might do! It was threshing day, and nothing else mattered to me! I pedalled my three wheeler trike, down the driveway to the main road many times that morning, straining for a better view of the direction the outfit would be coming from. Pup seemed somewhat perplexed by my constant back and forth on the driveway, but did not question my efforts by lagging behind. If his young master was excited, that likely meant some new wheels would be coming to sniff and wet for him as well! Mom sensed my impatient mood, serving me a lunch of watermelons and *roll-kuchen*. *Roll-kuchen* is a special dough made with lots of eggs (cracks in our case), some flour and milk, with a pinch of this and that. Then it's fried in hot oil on the fired up kitchen stove for about a minute, and, combined with watermelon, it's a real treat. That pinch of salt in the *roll-kuchen* does make the watermelon taste even sweeter!

Pup let a growl on the front steps that reminded me of today's mission and I was out the back door, with Mom's standard reminder to be careful and stay out of the way! "How can you stay out of the way when you are in the main cast of the show," I thought, but dared not ask. I did not want any flawed adult logic, or even common sense, to get in the way of my plans. Pup had given me a false alarm and after checking the road, with no outfit in sight, we both wandered back to some shady trees. I hauled out the pocket full of warm *roll-kuchen* I had plundered on my hasty retreat from the table. Was I glad for large overall pockets! Pup claimed his portion by creeping up close to my face as I was trying to eat my ill-gotten gain! His bad breath, once he got up close and personal, will cause you to recall the agreement you have with him! An amendment to that sharing agreement with Pup about backing away after he had his share of the pillage was an oversight of major proportion on my behalf!

Already a rustle of leaves beneath the large poplar tree. The hot sun plus the contentment that *roll-kuchen* and watermelon do provide in a young man's tummy, I must have fallen asleep, for I woke with a start! Pup's tummy had moved with his first woof! Since my head was on his outstretched anatomy, I felt his muscles bounce with his bark. Pup was always with me, and, while we both seemed to enjoy that arrangement, he was also a liability for me. Mom had learned that, to find out where and what I was up to, she gave out a demanding whistle. Pup was my true friend, but even Pup knew not to ignore Mom's whistle (she fed him most often) and went running to her. The direction Pup came from for the most part blew any camouflage I might have had on my covert activities! Today however Pup just moved because his special sensitive dog's ears had heard a new sound, and once we were on the driveway, I saw what Pup had heard.

The huge, huffing and puffing D John Deere was heading our way with the thresher in tow, half a dozen teams of horses and hayracks behind him. Some racks were already being loaded in our fields. I felt like giving Mom a "heads up" that the outfit was here but my second thought overrode this thoughtful idea. If I go to the house and tell Mom, I likely won't be able to complete my plan!

The big D tractor was belching smoke as if to announce he was arriving. I could now feel the vibrations on the ground under my bare feet. The vibrations came from the steel cleats that were attached to the large rear tractor wheels. These cleats dug into the ground for traction as the clumsy "steel horse" was trying to hurry along. The cleats left a trail of dug up dirt at its top speed of three miles per hour. I was well out of the range of Mom's voice or even whistle; my plan was working!

As the outfit pulled up closer, I was wearing my best PR smile for the gang master, driver of the outfit.

I knew he would remember me from last year and he did, as he eased off the gas lever and pulled the large lever back to stop the outfit. An invitation, if it came, was redundant, as I was already climbing onto the back platform of the big D. The gang master was standing and I slid into the tractor's steel seat before the gang master could say "How are you?" "What will I call you this year?" I asked. "Just call me Mr. Dan as they all do," he replied. Calling a person by their correct name was very important in the Mennonite values of life. Each person must be respected, my parents had drilled into me, and calling the person by the correct name was respectful. My tact in blurting out the question to Mr. Dan might not have received my mom's approving look, but I wanted to clear up the matter early and Mom was not present to admonish me!

Mr. Dan had now pushed the lever forward and we were underway, while the second lever brought us to full speed. I had noted every lever move Mr. Dan had made in putting the tractor in motion, in case I would be allowed to—perhaps be called upon—I could make the correct moves later, during threshing. Pup, who had immediately wetted the wheels of the hot machine, was now running alongside the outfit wagging his fluffy collie tail, knowing I was in good hands, meaning also that his job of escorting me was going well! As we approached our yard I noticed out of the corner of my eye Mom watching us draw nearer.

My memory bank told me it would be risky to make eye contact with Mom, for a disapproving look from her could also be noted by Mr. Dan. This would surely convey a contrary message that I did not want at the start of his and my likely week-long relationship. I was busy chatting up Mr. Dan as we crossed our yard and was quick to jump off the tractor to open the barb wire gate that led to the pasture and the remains of last years straw stack, where the outfit would again set up.

I was bent on proving my value to the gang master. His approval would not only allow me to sit on the tractor's seat while threshing, Mr. Dan could also help my seating arrangement at the dinner table with those muscle-bound men! Threshing to me was a "men's game" and even the seating arrangement at our dining room table was part of that macho game! After all, how can a young man be taken seriously if he is not to mingle and sup with the best! Whether I ate at the first, second or the dreaded third table setting, Mr. Dan could influence the seating arrangement with a wink at Mom, a small pushover of his chair and share the wide berth Mr. Dan was given at the table, which could nicely accommodate me. An eating spot alongside the master, it just does not get any better than that for the newest and youngest member of the gang!

The scars from last year's threshing dinner table seating arrangement was still fresh in my mind! I had mauled and remauled that cruel event in my mind during the past year and was determined not to repeat that bitter event this year! The route to becoming "a somebody" was to be able to eat at the first table, where Mr. Dan sat! Last year I had been relegated to the third table setting, which had included a few men, Mom and my sisters! That was kitchen staff! I was in the threshing gang! That nightmare had to be corrected and the time was now! These days were the "threshing Olympics" to me! I was determined to stand on the center stage, when the "threshing anthem was sung" each day! My plan was to be in the good books of Mr. Dan and of course not cross up Mom and Dad—especially Mom, who could be influenced by a pesky sister! To help the "Mom's side" of the PR game, I did help gather the eggs the day before, without a fuss. The hen's hooked sharp beak seemed like a magnet to my hands. Often when alone on these egg gathering trips I had a secret stick that I brought to the hen house and when that grumpy hen wanted to peck me, I gave her a jab with the stick, which sent her squawking and complaining across the yard. If questioned, I was as puzzled as anyone as to the fuss the old hen was making! But today was different! I suffered the beak pecks in silence, gathering the eggs that Mom would need for boiling tomorrow's part of the snack and main meal as well, for the hungry threshing giants! Running messages was another way of keeping my PR "brownie points" with my folks.

For now I was fully engrossed with the task at hand, and that was to get the threshing machine and tractor positioned for threshing. Mr. Dan and his assistant Tommy walked about the old straw stack, checking wind direction for a suitable site for the outfit to set up. The old straw stack served a purpose all year. In winter we got our bedding straw for the cattle from here and in late fall and early spring, when the cattle was allowed outside again after a long winter cooped up in their barn stalls. The cattle would love to run and brush against the settled straw stack, to get that itchy extra hair off or just a general itch session. As well, should the weather deposit a sudden squall, the animals would find shelter from the winds. The site for the threshing outfit, having been decided upon. The skills of the gang master would now be tested and displayed. The threshing machine was backed into place, favourable to the wind. But it must now be anchored, so that when the long seventy foot belt that drives the thresher and stretches from the huge three foot diameter pulley on the thresher to the modest two foot pulley on the tractor and get full tension without either machine moving. To secure the thresher, the wheels had been dropped into an eight-inch breech in the ground. Again, with the skills of Mr. Dan, the big D was so positioned that thresher and tractor were facing each other. That heavy, seventy foot belt, likely near two hundred pounds, was placed over both pulleys and the tractor backed till the tension on the belt, which had been criss-crossed forming a figure eight look from the side, would drive the thresher without any belt slippage. This procedure required the experience of a man that had been trained for years under a veteran gang master and now Mr. Dan was in the prime of his career.

The pulley lever on the big D was eased forward, the gentle giant put the thresher, with its near hundreds of belts and chains, into motion. Tommy climbed the vertical steel ladder onto the thresher, and inspected the slow churning machine. He adjusted the straw blower, by cranking it from its moving-resting position, all the way from pointing to the front and now pointing to the rear of the thresher, where the straw was to land on the huge stack to come. Applying full throttle, Mr. Dan checked the RPM (revolutions per minute) on the thresher, to be sure there was no belt slippage and this check was repeated many times throughout the day. Any deviation in RPM of the machine would effect threshing efficiencies resulting in grain ending up in the straw stack rather than the grain hopper. The tractor fuel supply had been topped up from the horse drawn supply wagon that carried several barrels of distillate, oil, and spare parts for the machines that were known to wear out during a threshing campaign. The gang master that kept his equipment in top-notch condition was a sought after boss, and Mr. Dan was such a master!

The load of sheaves had been waiting, the horses mildly nervous about new surroundings. The driver spoke softly to his team and that, plus the oat sheave I pulled from the rack and fed the horses, calmed them down, as one of them lowered his huge head and neck, nuzzling my cheek. The driver observed this from the top of his high fluffy load of sheaves and smiled, we had now also, along with the horses, formed a bond. Horses have long memories and when well treated will place their trust in you quickly. I have felt that next to a dog being men's best friend, the horse is a close second!

Mr. Dan raised his gray engineer's cap to the driver of the rack. The first sheaves went *thud* onto the thresher feeder trough. A trough about eight feet long and three wide, with a moving chain slat that fed the sheaves into the hacker blades that moved up-forward-down than back again. This motion cut binder twine that had held the sheave together and also some mulching of the sheave took place before being devoured by the giant machine wide cylinder. This cylinder is the basis for threshing as it rushed the sheave through a half-inch concave opening, tossing all back, where shakers and blowers separate grain from chaff. The straw and chaff was thrown through the blower tube some seventy feet through the air, forming a stack.

The pure clean grain had fallen through the shaker screens and augured to the side of the thresher, where the grain leg with its chain and scoops put the grain into the bushel bucket. The bucket was suspended on a hanging scale and once the desired weight of grain had been reached, a gate opened on the bucket, with the grain pouring into the waiting farmers wagon. Dad, who at other farms was a rack driver, was on his own farm now hauling grain from thresher to the granary on the farm with his team of horses and wagons.

The grain was scooped by hand with shovels and was a real biceps builder! While Dad was away with unloading one wagon of grain, another was filling at the thresher. When Dad returned with the empty wagon it was backed into place, the horses hitched to the full wagon, with the jockeying between wagons going on all day.

All things seldom go as planned! Here the crop was heavier than estimated and Dad was "in tough" to keep up with hauling the grain to the granary. Having to stop the threshing machine because the empty wagon was not back from unloading, with the waiting wagon heaping full of grain, brought a scowl to Mr. Dan's face. Time was precious, so to solve the problem a large hopper on huge steel wheels was brought in. The hopper was as tall as the thresher and the grain now flowed into the hopper, with a sloped floor.

Wagons side by side were backed to the hopper, a gate opened and in minutes a full wagon of grain. Even then Dad had to work into the night to empty the grain from the hopper, after threshing had long been halted for the night.

Mr. Dan knew of an available young man that had a team of horses and was able to relieve Dad of some of the grain hauling. Dad needed some time to mingle with the men and eat with them at mealtime. This also allowed Dad to communicate with Mr. Dan as to which field goes next, etc. While a large crop was a blessing of abundance, it also had its challenges!

I just loved this high hopper and was quick to climb the wooden vertical ladder to the top. From the hopper I had a bird's eye view of the entire outfit, and I allowed my mind to think I was in charge of the entire outfit! The view was mind boggling as the tractor, horses and racks, unloading as well as waiting to unload, were in my view and imaginary control. I savoured the thought, but did not verbalize it.

Mr. Dan had consulted with Dad and Mom as to the estimated threshing time for today, as the threshing time was decided by the dew setting in. Once the dew settled in, the threshing got tough and ineffective. With Mr. Dan, some twenty years of threshing experience, he could tell by the clouds, wind and his arthritic knee what weather Mother Nature would toss at us. By two o'clock Mr. Dan would tell the gang, "We will be running late tonight boys" and no one would doubt his call. Today however, with furled brow, he said to Mom "dew will come early, just a running lunch will do as we will have to shut down early tonight." He further added "doubt we will be running tomorrow, rain coming," as he eyed the western sky. Dad nodded in agreement, much to his chagrin.

A "running lunch" meant Mom and sisters would bring the lunch to the thresher and the men would eat on the run. Mom's running lunch was better than many farm's main course servings was, so said the men. The hand-pulled wagon of goodies arrived about 3:30, the men knew Mom's schedule well and by that time several racks were at the machine, rather early. The cooked eggs, sandwiches, always a ten gallon crock of sour dills, gallons of hot coffee, and that rich farm cream that with one dollop could turn a regular coffee into a latte! At some farms the so called "cream" looked thinner than our milk did but Mom's standards did not allow such cost-cutting measures and rich cream made the men's lips smack! Today she had added farmer sausage to the menu, as she felt the dew might just hold off a bit longer and she did not want "her men" to leave our farm hungry. "A well-fed person works best" was Mom's motto!

Mr. Dan and Tommy both found ample time to be at the lunch wagon. Mr. Dan would watch to make sure this did not happen to his rack drivers, as this could result in no loaded racks being back with sheaves to thresh. Many a driver would slip an extra sandwich into his chafey overalls pocket, as well as a dill pickle or two into his sweaty red bandana hanky, to eat as he was riding to the fields for another load.

Mom always remembered to pack a nice lunch for the "field pitchers" who moved from rack to rack in the fields, helping others load racks but were unable to come and enjoy the lunch wagons. The rack drivers took the lunch to the fields to some very grateful men! When these men did come to our house for a sit down dinner, they were sure to thank Mom and toss a wink. What goes 'round, comes 'round!

Mr. Dan, now having had at least two large coffees and sampled each of the offerings once or twice, allowed a healthy burp, still watching to be sure the drivers remain in their proper rotation. The drivers knew Mr. Dan was watching them and if they "dallied" a bit to much at the lunch wagon they would load their racks fast, but not as tall as normal, in order to remain in the correct rotation at the thresher, hoping Mr. Dan would not notice the smaller load. Mr. Dan did notice and as the driver was leaving to reload, Mr. Dan would motion to the driver to make his loads taller. Not much got past Mr. Dan's roving eyes, and while the driver may not have appreciated being reminded in front of other drivers, he knew he was guilty and this fact was not lost on him in the future.

Mom was right, the dew did hold off longer than Mr. Dan had predicted, and the threshing did go on a few hours longer, the extra heavy running lunch paid off well! Mr. Dan, being the gentleman he was, thanked Mom for the heavier lunch she had served, while she graciously accepted the compliment. Mom had been a student of threshing weather for many years and it showed in her predictions! We tucked into bed, rather pleased with the threshing progress. The rain did come, and threshing was off for the day at least. Those men living not to far from our farm had left their racks and ridden home on their team of horses. Those from a distance stayed and enjoyed Mom's breakfast, lunch and dinner. A few of the men could have gone home but they liked Mom's cooking, as well as the "cock and bull" sessions in the barn that were part of the day off. These sessions by and large were "yarns of the past!" Most stories seemed embellished some, others were to my young ears "well past the mark of possibilities!"

The story tellers, even though well embellished, kept a straight face while telling their yarn and each guy seemingly had to outdo the other guy's story! These yarns were told in the barn, (very appropriate) while sitting on upside-down pails or apple crates and I was sitting there on my little milk stool, taking it all in. Of course, for me to speak up or laugh at the yarns would have indicated I was catching on to the conversation, and that might have stifled the yarns, which I so much enjoyed! Mom and Dad's concerns that "sex education and vocabulary" might expand too rapidly were well founded! My fertile, inquisitive mind retained every new word and this was brought to our next visit to cousins and friends homes! This lead to extensive speculation amongst us growing lads, as to what it meant and if incorrect conclusions were arrived at, they could be corrected on the next visit. The world lay at our feet and we better get on with it, to allow our knowledge to catch up with our hormones!

My cousins' eyes rounded when I suggested the size of the pumpkins grown by one of the threshing men. The number of piglets a sow was supposed to have had caused some gasps! There were many more stories best left in the barn, and I will. But the one story claimed that he was pacing his stallion along a country road in his buggy, when the stallion sensed in his nostrils a mare in heat about a half-mile down the road. The story teller sitting on his upside-down pail, looked around to be sure he had everyone's attention. Satisfied that most were with him on this yarn, he carried on, "I lost control of the stallion, as he galloped wildly to the mare in heat!" Again he did a quick glance about before his punch line, "The stallion galloped so fast that the telephone poles were whizzing by me like it was a picket fence!" Most of the men in the story circle pushed back and sauntered away, either they had heard the story before or it was too far out of the realm of possibility to bother with.

Some decided to help Dad get more grain bins ready, while others did repairs on their racks and greased the wheels on their racks, as well as others left behind by other drivers. Helping each other was the Mennonite way! Later some had a nap in the hayloft after Mom's tasty lunch. The men were accustomed to sleeping in the hayloft of the farmer's barn. A strict no smoking policy was in place and respected, although in rare cases a driver was seen to smoke on top of his load of sheaves. Not within sight of Dad or Mr. Dan, as this was a real no-no as well! The drivers joked about mice running over their bodies at night when sleeping in the lofts. At our farm we had several cats on duty before the threshing season began and no such mice claims were made at our farm.

On the rainy days, some feats of strength and power could be seen taking place in the barn or granary. Arm wrestling, weight lifting and chin-ups were in the impromptu competition. It was revealing to me that oft' the smaller man, stature-wise, was the winner!

Later in the afternoon the sun came out beaming, the drying winds were blowing and Mom was already preparing next day's menu, when Mr. Dan declared that threshing would happen next morning, with a ten o'clock start likely, to allow a bit more drying time for the sheaves.

Since hydro was still "a city thing," it meant no fridges or freezers to draw food from for Mom. Hand labour and fresh from the garden was a given. I always felt that the women had the tougher task of having meals ready for the hungry men. Sure the men worked hard, but things were at a more given pace than the women's unpredictable meal requirements! Of course the food tasted better fresh from the garden but the pressure was on the host farmer's family to have meals timely and tasty. Dad was always quick to give the women credit for the large part they played in a busy, successful harvest! Fridges no, but we did have an ice house in the backyard, although the ice was now all but gone from the hot summer. This ice house was but a glorified dog house, about ten feet by the same, low hip roof, which covered a hole about the same size and also ten feet deep. It had a wooden lining and was filled with ice every November, with the blocks of ice cut and hauled from our dugout. The dugout was fenced in late August and the freezing action is a great purifier of water. Therefore when the ice was about two feet thick, Dad and some neighbours came with axe, a huge saw with ugly large teeth plus it was eight feet long. The axe chopped a hole in the ice, than the ugly saw was stuck in and the up and down of the saw cut chunks of ice three feet wide and six feet long or thereabouts. These ice blocks floating in the open steaming water were now pulled out with equally ugly ice tongs. The tongs set, the men locked shoulders and on the count of three the front end of the ice block peeked over the ice edge. Another heave-ho and the entire block was there to be picked into smaller chunks. The picking apart was simple, a blow from the axe and the ice blocks were ready. Ice sleds were used to haul the blocks to the ice house and packed close together, filling it to the top. Sawdust covering did wonders to reduce the ice melting process. Most of our neighbours did not have an ice house and accepted that their cream would test sour at the creamery and reduce the price paid. My folks used the ice house and our cream tests came back "sweet."

As the ice slowly melted, the water seeped into the earth bottom but the getting into and out of the ice house was by ladder. The slope of the ladder changed as the ice melted. On this ice, meals, meat, milk, cream and soft drinks (now known as pop) were stored. Once eight years old, I became "in charge" of the ice house and learned to navigate the ladder well. I spread and re-spread the sawdust to be most effective in keeping the ice from melting too fast and the products stored cold. Being in charge also had its privileges. Dad bought the soft drinks (Wynola was the Coke of today) by the case, which was cheaper than the five cents a bottle per single price. It was my job to pack the pop bottles in the crevices and crannies to keep it cold. With my "squirrel mentality" I knew where to find the pop but not my siblings and oft (for good reason) was accused of being able to find just another bottle or two when Dad was thirsty, knowing that he shared well with me! Howls from the siblings fell on deaf ears for the most part, and I confess I also drank "the odd bottle" on the sly, as I rested in the ice house from my "cellar master duties!"

Mom was a great cook but also fortunate that Dad was a "Mom Pleaser!" Before the threshing season began, Mom had dropped a hint that a larger cookstove would be helpful in preparing the meals for the threshermen. Dad was always wide awake for a bargain and he knew of a nice larger stove with gleaming front chrome features, an eight hole top, and bake oven that held eight large pies at one baking. A bargain was struck and Dad came home with the new sparkling stove. Mom was thrilled that Dad had taken the bait and bought the cookstove. The former stove went into the summer kitchen, where the more messy items were cooked. The kitchen was connected to the house via a concrete sidewalk. Mom loved her new stove! The filling of the wood box at the end of the stove fell into my lap. I knew the right mix of wood to fill the box with. Oak was a slow burner that held the heat up well, while old shingles and poplar wood were the starters and quick action wood. At times some shelled corn cobs were still in the bin, and Mom loved them for almost quick gas heat. The wood bin filled, which was followed by my tummy. The action I could hear coming from the thresher hastened my breakfast and I was out the door in a flash!

The clanging I heard was from Mr. Dan and Tommy, replacing a chain on the thresher that had been suspect when last threshing. The big D was fueled up with yet another barrel of distillate, which was a cheaper by-product of gasoline. Mr. Dan seemed relaxed as he did his walk about on the as yet lifeless machines. The position of the thresher was not the best since the wind had changed directions a bit, but moving the outfit was always a risk while the wind was making up its swirly mind.

Mr. Dan was startled, a load of sheaves had arrived at the thresher and the outfit had not been fired up and checked out! He had lost track of time; as he pulled out the watch from his special pocket via the long gold chain, reality set in. It was ten o'clock and the boss is never late or wrong!

Mr. Dan whistled, and Tommy abounded and with one look knew Mr. Dan was not pleased! No battery required on the big D for starting. In fact, batteries were not part of any make of tractor at that time that I was aware of. Starting most tractors was done by crank on the front crankcase. The D John Deere was the only tractor to have a fly wheel that was used for starting and once running, the balance the motor required. The flywheel was made of very dense steel, eighteen inches in diameter and three inches thick. Located just ahead of the rear wheel, with the flywheel shaft running through the tractor to the working belt pulley on the other side that drives the thresher. The pulley was always disengaged when starting the D. A clutch lever would be used to give purchase to the pulley's engine power. With only two cylinders, the flywheel kept the power even.

The big D burned distillate when running, but had to be started on regular gas. This involved another small gas tank and meant turning this tap, draining that *gismel*, and finally, without the careful procedure Mr. Dan normally used, he gave the fly wheel a hefty spin, hoping to save time. Then another spin and another spin, without the D even making an effort to fire up! A few more turns of frustration and Mr. Dan said "It's flooded!" A few choice words were expressed but Mr. Dan was a gentleman and restrained himself from saying more, although his lips were twitching! Flooding meant the excess gas sucked into the firing chamber would have to drain away and that would take at least twenty minutes. A second load of sheaves rode up behind the first waiting one, and Mr. Dan did take note!

While he and myself did have a good relationship, now was not the time for me to be close or ask questions! I noticed my sister pull up with a loaded wagon of goodies. The waiting men scrambled from their racks and poured coffee, reaching for the goodies with the other hand. With their large hands two or three items fit just right in their palms! I remembered that Mr. Dan was fuming behind the tractor and would not show up for the coffee wagon and risk a testy question or remark from the men. Yes, he had been careless in losing track of time but his pride was alive and well!

I had noticed his coffee liking the other day and his larger than the rest of the mugs was still there. I filled it, leaving room for that "oops" of rich cream, that I knew he liked. Several snacks on an empty glass saucer and the large mug of coffee, I surprised him as I rounded the big D! A quick glance at me, without a word, he reached for the mug with his brawny brown arm, the mug with the extra large ears, another quick look at the cup as if to say "this little rascal does not miss a trick!" I placed the saucer on the back of the D platform. A big swig from the mug as he smacked his lips, reaching for the goodies on the plate. I thought I heard a muffled "Thank you!" Mission accomplished, I took exit without a word. The other men were not as alarmed about the delay, as they sipped a second or third cup of java and balanced the sips with a cheek full or two of the snacks! My Sis had brought cool aid and so my coffee hopes looked bleak. When she turned her back to watch another rack of sheaves drive up, I made my move and headed for the tractor with my coffee cup in hand! Sisters can so crimp the style of a budding farmer!

Now a big spin on the flywheel and the D belched smoke from openings I did not know he had! The distillate valve was turned and the tractor hissed but accepted the new fuel without further fuss. "Give the lever a push" was the command to me, as I happened to sit on the big D! Mr. Dan proceeded to do his walk about, as my lever push had activated the entire thresher. All systems were go, with Mr. Dan nodding at me as I gave the tractor its full power! He raised his gray cap to the rack driver and threshing had commenced.

I was thrilled to bits! Mr. Dan had trusted me with the levers to start the threshing and all the men had noticed! The coffee had paid dividends quickly, I thought! As Mr. Dan passed by the big D, where I was still sitting smug, he gave my shoulder a hard squeeze and said, "We will have a busy day, son!" I knew I had impressed him.

Years later Mr. Dan bought a more powerful gas guzzler of a tractor, called a Hart-Par. Some more power, but all gas and the Hart-Par had its exhaust pipe come out from below the crankcase in front and shooting its fumes forward rather than up and out like the D did. During the day all was well, but when dusk and darkness set in the Hart-Par would shoot out fumes and flames, complete with fireballs of unburned gas. While pretty to watch, some horses did not appreciate the fireworks and certain teams required a man to hold them by their bridles and speak comfort to them. They got used to the flame-thrower in time and all was back to norm. It should also be said that some rack drivers brought on the flame-throwing knowingly, as a lark. They would pitch sheaves very fast, causing the Hart-Par governor to kick in and supply extra gas to meet the energy requirements of the extra sheaves being tossed. Now more unburnt gas was thrown out and caused the fireballs to increase. A quick walk to the rack by Mr. Dan got the relax message and things settled down. Some of these thresher guys were "young bucks" that enjoyed a bit of razzle-dazzle that the older men thought foolish! Also when walking past the front of the Hart-

Par, day or night, one had to respect the exhaust pipe in front or your trousers would be shot skyward!

Back to the here and today! The drivers were a bit extra aggressive this day and the big D belched extra smoke to protest, but to no avail. The drivers had lost a day of threshing and catching up was their goal. Big D suffered in near silence but gobbled up extra fuel and continued to belch smoke for the unrequested workload! Mr. Dan noticed the extra efforts from the drivers and trusted they would slow up a tad and not plug up the thresher. This would not only be further downtime but unclogging the thresher was a dusty, stifling job inside the near air proof surroundings. Mr. Dan had placed a can of tar near the hot exhaust on the D to let it warm up and liquefy some. Now he drizzled the warm tar on the whirling drive belt to be sure there was no slippage between tractor and thresher. The tar remained on the belt for days, making a hissing, clicking sound noise on the pulleys. The smoke belching proved a bit much for Mr. Dan and he gave the driver a stare, with the message received by the rack men, both pitching and watching how the big D kinda smirked with a few big puffs as if to say, "I told you I would tell!"

When a rare dispute occurred between farmer and gang master, the center of controversy was the setting of the bushel counter. Wheat, when ideally grown, weighs sixty pounds per bushel. While oats weighs in at thirty eight pounds. It is, however, the norm to have grain weigh in at less than the ideal due to growing conditions and etc. The gang master has an "official" sized pail that he uses for weighing the grain at a new farm and then sets the bushel scale accordingly. The master is paid by the bushel and the oftener the bushel counter trips, it's more money in the master's overalls. Weight of grain can and does change from one spot on the field to another. The frazzled farmer felt the bushel weight was not checked often enough and the master was taking advantage of him. With thousands of bushels threshed in a day, the difference can be quite a bit. To me, Mr. Dan was a fair man, checking the grain weight often. Dad never had any run-ins with the gang master. They had worked together for many a year and they trusted each other. One time the bushel counter broke when threshing on our farm. Rather than stop threshing, Mr. Dan and Dad agreed on the number of bushels in a wagon load, again both were fair and the threshing continued.

I was in the grain hopper, all was flowing well, when Tommy, on top of the thresher, gave me a nod. He had a makeshift chair and was known to nod off a bit, knowing I would see any problems and call him. For now he gave me a sleepy wink and it felt so good to be in charge! About twenty minutes later Tommy waved hello to me and again looked refreshed. Mr. Dan now climbed the ladder, while Tommy took the ground duties. In Tommy's makeshift chair, Mr. Dan also fell victim to the sandman, and he too had forty or so winks. Now it was my turn and I waved in adult style to Tommy, as I climbed down the hopper ladder to my waiting collie. Hand on his mane we walked to a shady tree but hidden from the gang. I lay down on Pup and dozed off like a switch had been thrown!

The crack of lumber woke Pup and me. It was Dad's new hired man, having been a bit testy with his team, and had broken the wagon tongue while backing an extra heavy load of grain to the bin. Dad knew this could put pressure on the one remaining wagon and I scooted back to the hopper and spread the grain so that if there was a delay in hauling, the hopper could hold more grain. A replacement tongue was available on the supply wagon and installed without losing much time. With the later start and the wagon feast the men had had, he decided that the noon sit-down meal should be one o'clock. Mom complied but she was not pleased. To her, the noon meal, Mennonites call dinner (the six o'clock meal is supper), was to be at eleven-thirty, but she went along with Mr. Dan on this occasion.

By one o'clock it was amazing how many racks "just happened" to be on our yard. The men were hungry and Mom did not disappoint! The aroma on the yard just caused the men to stop and this caused a jam up at the first table. Mr. Dan and myself saw the jam up and we waited for the second table. I noticed that after the men had taken healthy seconds, they decided to pass on Mom's warm pies. That is until the first guy took a slice into his plate and passed on the pie. Down the line it went and came back empty. Another rhubarb pie was sent down, and it too came back empty. These men were expending a huge amount of energy and a few hundred calories extra were not a problem. In fact, the word calorie had not been uttered in Mennonite circles at that time!

The men were again loading or unloading their racks. I had my fill at the second table with Mr. Dan and some other men. Mr. Dan took his pie and sat down with Mom in the kitchen area where she too was snacking. They were laughing and enjoying the conversation I could tell. It was high praise indeed when the gang master would sit down with the hostess, sharing time and dessert. The men noticed and knew he was speaking on their behalf as well. Mom's face was glowing as she listened, in her clean fresh apron, her hair neatly done, she looked like the threshing queen she was!

Mr. Dan made his move back to the thresher, allowing Tommy to come and dine. I walked with Mr. Dan as he released a heavy burp, while marveling at Mom's fine cook stove as we passed by. The large pot of potatoes, carrots and peas were all in the summer kitchen, leaving room on the new stove for coffee pots and those yummy pies. The fried meats were also done in the outside kitchen, with aromas filling the yard, causing drivers to drool as they rode by even after just having enjoyed a meal. The gravy over the spuds and the meat was a rare treat, simply drippings from the fried farmer sausages, add some rich cream, pinches of pepper, spoon of flour to thicken the plot, salt, and most men's dreams are happening!

The huge pots of noodle soup was made the day before and re-heated today. The second heating is when noodle soup is at its peak! The blending, maturing and marinating actions of the fine ingredients takes about twenty-four hours to happen. This gives the soup the spice taste it deserves!

As a change of pace, when the day was perfect Mom had the long pig cutting table brought from the granary. This was but thick boards fitted together to make a table four feet wide and ten feet long. Placed on low sawhorses gave it the right table height. A spare table cloth was rolled over the top, the table under a still, shady tree, the men were impressed as they gathered round. Another shorter table was quickly added and sixteen men bowed their heads to say grace. The light breeze just rustled the drying leaves a bit, giving it the picnic feel Mom had been striving for! The men were overwhelmed with the effort put forth by Mom and her crew and did not mince words in saying so!

In years after, Mom was often asked if the outside meal was coming again, as it had been a memory for all. Mom did accomodate these requests another time I recall.

Some school chums rode by on their bikes, asking me to join them in some skinny dipping in the local creek. I explained my duties would not allow me to join them, as I wiped some sweat. As I lay back in the hopper, my tummy reminding me that one piece of pie would have been just right, I was swept back when Mom was but a young lass. I loved it when Mom would regale me with stories of her youth. Mom came from a very large family, sixteen the count! The first nine were girls, meaning a few would have to help on the large farm, doing a man's job. At age twelve, Mom would take a team of four horses and plow with them all day. At threshing time she was pitching sheaves with the grown men. By all accounts, she not only held her own well, but was the one to set the pace that men have told me they struggled with!

While the threshing machine had not changed that much from Mom's time, the engine supplying the power had changed, big time! The steam engine was the power of Mom's day! The gas combustion engine had not been invented yet or at least not in mass production. The steam engine, a lumbering beast, would dwarf the big D. As there were several sizes of steam engines, the comparison of power from steam engine to the big D is somewhat like comparing apples and oranges. By all accounts the steam engine was very powerful, especially when in the hands of an experienced steam engineer, or steam operator as they were often referred to. A mild power comparison between the big D and the large steam engine would be that the D walks along with four ploughshares and a large steam engine would huff along with twelve ploughshares!

Being a steam operator was considered a full-time job and a lot of pride was evident in holding this position. The gang master and the steam operator were two separate duties and persons. The cooperation between the two men was, however, largely the difference between a so-so threshing gang or a top-notch crew.

The reason for the full time job of making steam was that the engine boiler held about fifteen minutes worth of steam (depending on boiler size). A steady feed of heat was required to keep the steam at the umteen level, not under supply, nor over. Under supply and the gang master would be compelled to shut down threshing due to low RPM. Over supply of steam would mean blowing this unused energy into the air; both were major embarrassments to the steam operator. The steam engine had a pressure gauge and redlining that gauge would leave a lot of lives in danger. Boilers could and did blow up, with loss of lives.

So for the steam operator, there was no hiding his errors if he was lax in his duties. Some operators seemed to have a special knack to keep the steam just purring along. It then appeared his job was the soft touch as he carried on conversations seemingly all day. The not-so-gifted an operator seemed to be sweating it all day! Blowing the steam off into the air was subject to a lot of mocking the operator. Men on the racks would stand and raise their hats in mock celebration. Steam guys have been know to miss a meal rather than being roasted at the meal table with the hostess present!

The steam engine could be fed with a variety of fuels, it was simply a case of placing whatever fuel you choose to under the belly of the huge water boiler, which than turned into steam when sufficent heat was applied. The oft most fuel used was straw (often just threshed straw now hauled to the steam engine) oak wood old lumber or used rail road ties. Old tree stumps were also hauled in when a blazing fire was happening and lots of steam called for in the next few hours.

Stopping the thresher was the gang master's call. At times some nasty looks were exchanged between the gang master and steam operator when the gang master stopped the thresher. The steam operator felt they could have kept on threshing, even if the RPM's were down a bit, but would recover quickly with the quick heat fuel straw he was now feeding the engine. For the most part harmony existed between these two, as they knew they were "the catcher-pitcher," duo of this team, with winning their goal!

If the capacity of the engine and thresher were well matched, (thresher sizes varied as well as steam engines) it was common the feed the thresher from both sides of the feeder trough. The bushel counter was then humming and tripping, with the grain transporter requiring extra men and teams to haul the grain. Distance to haul the grain was also a factor, as threshing sites were not always on the farmer's yard close to the granaries. Many times the outfit, at the request of the farmer, set up the outfit on the farmer's field close to the sheaves. Nice for the rack men but more work for the grain haulers. The grain haulers with tall but narrow wagon wheels sank into the softer field earth, making the horses work harder and at times less than full loads of grain to make the pull lighter.

Once the farmer had offered free straw to workers and neighbours and their were no takers, than the straw stack received the lit match after the thresher pulled out.

Moving the steam engine from one field to another was a time consuming undertaking. Aside from lost threshing time, it required some planning from the steam operator. A full boiler of steam before setting out to the next field, which could be miles away, was a must. When the steam ran low, he had no choice but to stop the outfit and rebuild the steam. Some steam engines had a metal open tank slung under its belly and this allowed tar soaked rail road ties to be burning before the trip began and would keep up the steam required till next set up location. Three miles per hour was top speed for the steamer.

The amount, of water required to quench the thirst of this behemoth engine was draining to say the least. Horse and wagon team, or teams, depending on the distance to the water source. Again the skill of the steam operator was critical to not allow too much cold water to enter the boiler. This could reduce the water temperature and steam supply, so while it appeared the steam operator had lots of time for coffee and talk, which a good operator did, but he had to be alert all the time. The pride of working "a perfect day"—meaning no stoppages—drew compliments at the dinner table and at times from the hostess, who seemed to be aware of the threshing news but was stuck in the kitchen!

Steady, steady, good boys (even if they were girls), was what brought me back to the here and now from my comfy dream world in the hopper! I scrambled down the hopper ladder in a flash and rounded the big D, comforting the team of spooked horses in record time! A stray cat, meaning no harm, had wandered by, likely checking out the straw stack for a mouse or two but the horses took offense. I grabbed the bridle of the one horse and began to stroke its nose softly, telling him that all would be well and this was just a big misunderstanding. The other horse nipped at my straw hat, reminding me that he too required some calming down. I stroked his nose as well and then went for some oats, feeding them from my hand. The horses quivering lips sucked up the oats, leaving me with a somewhat wet hand as a "thank you!" The next team had a pair of foals at mothers side. With the mare's approval, I was able to touch and pet the rather skittish young foals who much preferred to prance about but staying close to mom. Feeding time was anytime for them and likely won the trophy for most coffee breaks, with Mr. Dan a close second, but Mr. Dan's came from the coffee wagon!

The days turned into a week, and the talk from the drivers was, "Another few hours and your fields are cleaned out!" My feelings to the "near finished" comments were "half and half." It had been a great week, but the other half said, "It's also about as much as a young thresher of four years old can handle." Feeling "in charge" of such an operation did have a draining effect on a guy!

Already I saw some racks loading in the neighbours field, Mr. Dan motioned for me to pull back the levers on the big D one final time. As I did so, the thresher's motion came to a halt, and Dad backed up his grain wagon for the last load.

Mr. Dan was all business, had the thresher hooked to the D in no time. I rode with him on the tractor to the yard, a quick squeeze on the shoulder, thanks were exchanged, as well as a "see you next year," and the outfit grew smaller down our driveway!

House/barn where the author was born in!

The Quack of Thunder

*A*ll through the thunderstorm, my little brain was concerned about me not having shut the small door on the duck house. I had a small family of ducks: mom, dad and half dozen ducklings. A shack about three feet high in front, with a slanted roof to the back, about four feet wide and deep served as home to my quacky clan. The ducks seemed happy with the arrangement and I was rather proud to "have my own flock." At least it was my flock, if only to take care of. Once they were ready for market, it seemed they became "family property."

But for now things were well with my little world. I opened their little shack door, fed them—for which they thanked me over and over again each morning. I am assuming I was decoding their quacks correctly. I fed them some grain to jumpstart them, after that they found grasshoppers, slugs in our garden to meet their daytime food requirements. Plenty of water keeps ducks happy. At night, I again topped up their gizzards with some grain, which on occasion they would save for breaky next morning.

I assumed the insect and locust supply had been adequate during the day. Mom was happy to have the quackers rid our garden of unwanted pests. Ducks have good insect hunting sense, and it was fun to watch them operate in our garden. They are quick with their beaks and neck. A wayward grasshopper is no match for a duck's beak. Even the grasshopper jump seems to be read correctly by the ducks, as his earthly landing and end time come about the same moment!

Ducks are not as careful parents, however, as geese are, or so it seemed to me. The drake or papa duck seems to take the position that after he deposited the sperm in mama duck, his duties are for the most part as a family figure head after that. If danger lurks, mama quacks and the ducklings come running. If mama detects a duckling missing, the drake concurs that as a formality! If mama wants more ducklings, well, yes he will go along with that process. This of course requires another breeding session and incubation, primarily mama's duties as the drake sees it! While incubating the eggs, which is mama's job, he will consider sitting on the eggs so she can stretch her legs and flap her wings, providing he is sleepy at the time. If a duckling goes missing, a full-scale search is conducted by the rest of the gaggle, most times the youngster is found and rejoins the noisy flock for a huge celebration.

Duck parents, seem to allow for the fact that some "shrinkage" in ducky numbers will happen. If a little quacker gets lost in the weeds and stays behind, a cursory search by the parents—mostly mama, and the little guy is written off as "missing in action." On several occasions when I did my roll call in the evening feeding, finding the numbers did not balance from the morning statistics, a search party set out to find them. Pup and myself were the main (only) participants in this search party. We scoured the deep weeds surrounding the garden fences. We, or should I say I, did my best imitation duck quack, then listened for a response. At least on several occasions this did bring about quacky replies and Pup with his sharp ears honed in on the huddling little critter. Seems the little feller had resigned itself to spend the night in the weeds, not concerned about the roaming skunks and badgers that look for a late night snack. A little duck would be gourmet eating and, if he was not devoured, the chances of him meeting up with his family before becoming dehydrated were slim. A duck needs to wet his beak on a regular basis it seems. I picked up the cuddly little peeper, carrying his shivering body to the duck house. A quacky reunion did happen but as for my efforts, great quacks of gratitude were never expressed as I understood them. The little guy had a good drink of water, than disappeared under mama's wings for a night in the shed.

On the night of the thunderstorm however, I had not yet shut the duck house door for night.

All through the crashing thunder, I thought of my little quackers and how they were handling the situation.

After Dad had done his walk about the yard when the storm seemed to have passed, I again mentioned my concern for my brood. The sky, despite dusk setting in, had actually brightened up a bit. Dad gave the approval for me to hurry to the duck house and close the door. Likely the permission was granted to get me off his mind, which had bigger concerns to deal with.

The rain had begun falling softly but I would just hurry to get my concern looked after.

The ducks were in the shed as I reached for the small door, when a huge lightning bolt lit the sky and a thunderbolt joined it! I found myself on the seat of my pants in the duck compound!

Dad came running and we scampered into the house together, with me in full-blown tears!

The large tree had been struck again or what was left of it! The scare I got from the lightning bolt never did leave me, leaving my fieldwork at the slightest hint of an electrical storm brewing. Lightning chases and strikes the highest object in the area was the going theory at the time and on a flat open field, I was the highest object on the tractor, with the implement the tractor was pulling acting as the ground, a requirement to get killed!

As for my duck family, they came through the summer rather well, with only three duckies going missing in action. This left us a nice family to harvest duck down from.

Our family had learned that it was not wise to inform me as to when the duck family would be taken to market. The ducks had become a part of me and no explanation satisfied me as to why they should not all stay on the farm for the winter. I of course lost that battle every fall! The fortunate part was I moved on with life in a few days, and attached myself to another creature on the farm!

Anna the Iron Lady

*I*n reflection, I have heard it said many times that a certain person can have a great influence on one's life, but one is not as cognizant of that influence till later in one's life.

In hindsight, Anna Bergen was such a person in my life. Growing up only a short walk from the Bergen's large farmyard certainly will have affected this influence. Meeting and getting to know her is one of my first recollections other than my family.

Anna was a self-made person, or so it seemed to me. To my knowledge, Anna had only attended public school briefly. Her education, while for the most part confined to her family farm, came from her inner self.

A keen student of the Bible, Anna seemed to get her fill of the world news that counted, to her at least, from the German newspapers *Rundschau* (look-around) and *the Stienbach Post*.

Anna's knowledge of politics and current events was likely limited. But ask Anna about the mission fields, the missionaries, the upcoming events of the churches, more so the Mennonite Brethren ((MB) churches, and Anna held her own rather well.

Anna, a tall thin person, looked a tad frail perhaps, but that was very misleading! At home in a dress, never saw her in slacks, some rubber boots, and her graying hair in a bun. Anna's figure and fashions never did help grace the front page of any magazine! Even *the Farm and Ranch Review* magazine never honoured her with a visit! The few dresses she did have were washed and rotated in a monotonous routine!

Anna lived with her Mom and Dad on a large farmstead, some 200 yards from our home but was separated from our farm by a narrow, non-government maintained road. Thus the road had deep ruts at times, with the term "cow path" very fitting.

Our pasture's barb wired fence ran some 200 yards alongside their barb wired pasture fence separated by this glorified ditch we called a road. Our respective horses disagreed from time to time and fence repairs were a common need as the horses decided to kick at whatever they perceived as enemy or relieve pent up frustrations. Horse arguments need no reason, they commence without reason, and they also cease without one. Our neighbour's bull however was straightforward with his reason. Whenever the bull broke their fence and did so again with our fence, "It was our cow's fault," reasoned the opinion-ated Mr. Bergen!

Our cow "had beckoned" his bull and he had only answered her request. The bull's reasoning was transparent, nature's call, not so for horses!

Beard Bergen was Anna's father's moniker. Handles, monikers or nicknames, call them what you will but name them the Mennonites did! Beard Bergen came by his handle honestly, a long bushy white beard he had, with a tinge of yellow here and there as if he was a smoker and something was smoldering in that great white forest. A smoker he was not, at least to my knowledge. His full bib overalls, covering the standard plaid shirt, which covered an ample girth, a pocket watch he drew out often, as though he was on a tight schedule. Mrs. Bergen was a small, frail, kind lady, where Mr. Bergen had a tad of brashness about him. Our visits to the Bergen home were not frequent but more often than they at our house.

Mennonite tradition called for the "younger to visit the elder" folks more often. Mrs. Bergen, her head was always covered with a good, head-sized shawl or babushka. Her dresses were mostly in some shade of black! The Bergen's house and large barn were combined, as was ours in my younger years. The Bergen house and barn combination, however, remained in tact till it was reduced to rubble many years after I flew the Flatfields coop.

In summer, the front door of the house was used as a direct entry point. Come winter, you entered through the musty barn and then into the house. Not that my nose was unaccustomed to the barn smell!

It was the eyes that had the bigger task. At best, in a sunlight day, it was eerie walking towards the house entry through the barn as one had to. On a darker, cloudy day, thinking your way through was your only option.

The entry to the house was a messy area. Mr. Bergen was a "save everything" kind of guy, "Could come in handy, you know." The shelves, as far as I could tell, held as much useless items as they could hold! The barn floor was uneven, with a mixture of wooden planks and concrete to traverse over. The aisle, if that was what I think it was—it did lead to the house door, had silent spectators of pails, milk benches, pitchforks, pumpkin cutting machine lining the sides. Silent, I say, until your toes stepped just slightly out of bounds, then the spectators clanged and banged!

Mr. Bergen, when I got to know him, was not in the "absorbing of knowledge stage of his life." He had been there, done that and was now, however, quite willing to part with his acquired wisdom and he had acquired plenty! Simply put, he was a stubborn ol' codger! In another chapter you can read of the ongoing feud Mr. Bergen chose to have with our dog.

When you are young, all older people's homes have a distinct musty smell to them. The lineaments, the *Alpencruter*, the "comfort salves" all mingle, linger, permeate the curtains, the tablecloth and whatever else can absorb odor, the kerosene lamp oil the predominate bouquet!

Even the blooming houseplants did not send a fresh smell. The plants seemed to have made or called a truce with the aroma department, which seemed to be "We won't release our pleasant fragrance into this atmosphere, but we will not take part in any absorption plan either!" So the geraniums bloomed away like big, puffy cheeks on a kid with a secret but refused to share it.

Cushions or toss pillows were everywhere, on chairs, wooden sleeper bench, couch, but these had regretfully not entered into a "no odour absorption" contract! The fancy embroidery on the pillows were, by now, showing all the signs of old age, much like the Bergens!

So while I had reason to visit the Bergen farmyard often, mail, groceries; it was a situation where Mr. or Anna met me at the door when their dumb dogs roared! Items were given, at times exchanged, but never an invitation into their home when I was by myself.

As a kid I rather enjoyed visiting at the Bergen's on a once every year basis or so. I would have liked to investigate the upstairs but that invitation never came. The wooden cabinets in the dining-living room were intriguing. Small glass windows revealed some of the glass ornaments and wooden carvings that were special to Mrs. Bergen. She never did expound on any of these trinkets she valued, how she came into their possession, but to be sure, she knew they were there to stay as long as she did.

Mr. Bergen's words in almost all cases overruled the softer-spoken Mrs. Bergen's, at least in volume. However she picked her spots carefully and when Mr. was just too far out of line, in her humble opinion, she would raise her hand with a finger protruding and say, "*Vater, Vater*" (Father, Father). Mr. Bergen knew this was a good time to concede, which he did as gracefully as his ego allowed. He did not correct or interrupt as she put forth her thoughts. Even as an elder Mennonite lady, she was to be heard when it was called for, no women's lib required!

Pictures with Bible verses were generously hung where either nail or hook would support such an item. The Bergen's bedroom off limits to me, but when the door was left open I did eyeball it quickly. A huge headboard of metal tubing on the big bed, heavy looking blankets and tons of pillows, it did look comfy. Mr. Bergen for sleep, day nap or night time, always did wear black "pirate type" shades of solid black paper, with a rubber band holding them in place. These he placed over his eyes when it was night or nap time. Admitting he ever took a nap was a major concession for his pride. Once, when I had disturbed his noon nap when delivering their mail, Mr. Bergen answered the door with the "Jessie James" black paper shades on his forehead! He insisted on complete darkness for his sleeping needs, be it day or night.

The dim oil lamp lent an eerie feeling to any room. The glass cylinder stood tall but was in need of cleaning, which would have aided the light situation somewhat.

Mr. Bergen was the only one in the area to buy and store a 45-gallon drum of kerosene oil for the lamps. This caused us and others to come to his farm for the required liquid fuel our dim lamps insisted upon to brighten our homes. To Mr. Bergen, it was the visiting these occasions provided that made the storing of the barrel worthwhile, for us it was the convenience. As well oil containers had a way of seeping when in a sled, bouncing over hardened snow banks, making for a smelly ride to town and back. Mr. Bergen had a way of being sure you would share the latest news, as if you knew it, by being tardy about filling your oil container until he felt he had extracted as much information from you as you were capable of regaling, then your container was filled.

Alpencruter was a popular "medicine" that seemed to help a host of ailments, provided it was taken internally on a regular basis, meaning daily, with lifetime as a time frame. The dedication the "old folks" had to the *Alpencruter* medicine was mystifying to me as a youngster. That it was an "adult medicine" was firmly established in my mind by the parents, but the nudge-nudge, wink-wink that seemed to follow these brief propaganda information sessions caused me retain the word *Alpencruter* in my mind "for fuller review" at a later date. Parents, I had learned were, simply put, not very forthcoming with classified information. Further, it was always filtered truth, at least on the non-mainstream items of young life, such as *Alpencruter* and sex! The *Alpencruter* review actually presented itself sooner than expected, when an empty bottle was carelessly left on their barn shelf for my tender eyes to read the ingredient list. It was a rare, bright sunny day when I came upon the required information for my study. Staring at me was the ten percent alcohol factor listed in bold print right on the bottle! Ah yes, now it became clearer to me, Mr. Bergen had lamented with a sigh, that while *Alpencruter* was to be "a bottle a month" medicine, Mr. Bergen moaned that the bottle at times ran out before the month did! How this alcohol-laden medicine were permitted to be advertised in newspapers still confounds me. It did state that the contents were good for aiding bowel movements! Mr. Bergen and Dad were conversing when Mr. Bergen lowered his voice, I just knew it was time to hone in my ears on this matter. The lowered voice said that every September he orders his six month winter supply of Alpencruter, so as to be sure he will not have to worry about having roads blocked with snow drifts and the last bottle wearing down.

The Bergen family was "staunch MB church members" and the MB pulpit had strong messages on the "evils of strong drink" (as did most pulpits of all denominations of the day). *Alpencruter* did not seem to be on the pulpit agenda, despite the high alcohol factor listed on the bottle. Could it be that *Alpencruter* was good "medicine" for pastors as well as lay people? I grew up before my study was complete!

Years later I was to learn that *Alpencruter* sales were highest in North American Bible belt areas.

The Apostle Paul did say to Timothy that a little snort of wine was good for the tummy, did he not?

Alpencruter, I tried a semi-legal snort one time, had a root beer flavour but with an alcohol kick to it!

A bottle of this in my lunch bag while herding cows, it would not have mattered whether it was cows or cats you were attending too, I would have been three sheets to the wind! What ailments it corrected or prevented was never clearly defined, as it seemed to have personal values to each consumer. Mr. Bergen said he got a "winter's supply" in October each year, avoiding the dreaded mid-winter drought that short ordering could bring on! Fruit wines (home-brewed) were also mentioned in conversations with Dad, but a sample was not offered to me for a youthful opinion! I digress!

Anna had an infectious smile, always. Whether Anna was in high rubber boots in barn muck or she was teaching my Sunday school lesson, when I did not always behave well as little boys are prone to do, a smile was a standard feature with her.

Anna was not a "good little Mennonite" girl that stayed in the kitchen and learned to cook. Food was not a tasty thing to her, food was grub to stay alive, not to be enjoyed, sustenance is the word! Anna ate to live, whereas I lived to eat. I cannot recall a single comment from Anna that she had enjoyed the meal or snack at our house, with my mom a five-star Mennonite cook!

We never took that as an insult, Anna simply ate only to nourish her body! As a kid who inhaled food, I could not help but wonder if indeed God had forgotten to give her any taste buds!

Outside in nature was where Anna was at home. The Bergens had not one but three large gardens, acres of produce! To help take care of these gardens, livestock and anything else, like repair kicked-down fences by the horses, the Bergen's had Tommy. Tommy, it seemed, had come to them as an orphan young lad or parents that were unable to care for him, at about age fourteen. In Mennonite circles some questions were not meant to be asked. This struck me as such a question, after about the third try to get a straight answer, I conceded defeat! Later hints suggested Tommy was not drawing any wage. This scenario of labour for roof and meals was not uncommon in those days.

Tommy, from the little I knew of him—all by observation, was a serious, hard working lad. Tommy was about eight years older than I was and related to my older siblings but not to me. Tommy was never rude or harsh to me, he simply ignored me! The clothes, room and board he received seemed to meet his needs and was prepared to exchange daily labour for the necessities in life.

Anna worked well with Tommy. The gardens were well attended to and the fruits of their labour could be seen throughout the summer, fall and winter. Flowers and plants pretty much took care of the front yard garden, while the cucumber, melons and huge pumpkins were in the back gardens. Birds of all kinds were in abundance.

On Sundays, the church our family attended (Sommerfelder) had an early start and we were often near home when we met the Bergen car making its way to their (MB) church service. This suited me well, whenever I saw all the Bergens in the car. This meant that I had an hour or so to go see the Bergen gardens without concern of being noted. I wondered in later days why I had not freely asked for permission from Anna to enjoy their bountiful gardens, rather than be somewhat cloaked about being there. The best answer that comes to me is that being just a tad sneaky was rather fun and added to the mystique of the day. Anna, I know, would not only have given me permission but have felt honoured to have me think their garden was worth a young lad's time! Certainly our garden at home was nice but their older setting with larger trees and sheer volume of produce did entice me. Even then I rarely crossed the Bergen's front yard on my way to the gardens, which was in the way back of the huge yard. Bergens had "dumb dogs" in my opinion. Mostly confined to the barn they would raise a loud, prolonged racket when they heard my footsteps, which might attract my dad's attention. Dad did keep an eye on any disturbance on the Bergen farm.

So through the Bergen pasture I went, provided the lazy bull was lying down. If that appeared dangerous, then a third route was behind the front garden, behind machine sheds and high weeds where skunks were known to live, definitely my third choice.

Another consideration I had to take into account when crossing the Bergen's yard leading to the large gardens was the Bergen's small flock, dozen or less of Guinea fowl, the only ones I had seen in my young lifetime. Guinea fowl, about the size of a heavy farm laying hen, dark gray feathers with white spots, on the plump side and leaning towards a pheasant, some might say. It's a bird that is native to Africa, how the Bergen's came to have these rare birds, escapes me.

They did have young each spring, nested in the garden in a spot of its choosing. That the flock remained at about the same number, yet did have young, also befuddles me. Perhaps "Guinea under glass," add a healthy dose of *Alpencruter,* the dim oil lamp, the ol' boy did have an extra twinkle in his eye from time to time!

I rather enjoyed observing these fowl as they scratched in the garden non-stop. They also did act as a watchdog, of sorts. Any noise they decided was a disturbance called for a "chirpy chatter" all their own.

The males did have bright red cheeks and I felt both sexes were pretty as I took in several hours of their workday from the shade of the tall trees on Bergen's yard.

On rare occasion these very private creatures ventured into our farmyard in their scratching, grazing activities, but were easily spooked back to the Bergen yard when they saw me or Pup. Adept flyers they were and just glided back home in a gentle swoosh! I felt special to be able to see such rare birds.

Once in the well hidden back gardens, I headed for the "ammunition dump," a large gravel pile that had stones galore, perfect for my slingshot, that was always hanging from my back pocket. The birds here were accustomed to a sanctuary like setting, a menagerie. Anna picked no fights with any beasts, except skunks. Tommy was not a hunter by nature and Mr. Bergen could not be bothered. The sparrows and blackbirds were plenty and very tame. Robins and noisy woodpeckers held their own well. The number of birds that succumbed to my aim with the slingshot were rather few I admit, close calls were treated as a hit, providing endless excitement. Robins, doves and a few other species had no reason to fear us at all, off limits to hunting on our yard, I treated the Bergen yard with the same respect.

Once the birds caught on to my presence, I retired to admiring the garden wares, which were in abundance. Sure I sampled the raspberries, the huge gooseberries, as Anna would want me to do. But never did I smash a melon nor do any other damage. A smashed melon would be a dead giveaway that an intruder had been there and the short list of perpetrators would have my name near the top. Living in such close proximity to the Bergens would make me a top suspect, as farm intruders were very rare. With red-handed evidence like a smashed melon or two, my dad would curtail my freelance journeys and secondly, Anna would look me in the eye next Sunday morning in Sunday school class that she alone taught in our little schoolhouse. Thirdly, I had no destruction bent in me, curiosity, adventurous, bit of devil perhaps, but never one to damage someone else's property. My Dad, himself a curious type of guy, allowed me that trait without question, but I knew where the line was drawn without ever testing his tolerance in damaged goods, others or ours.

There is a time to be brave, a time to be smart and the latter ruled when the risk to price ratio was this high. The rows and rows of pumpkins, which grew to three feet in diameter, were hauled into the barn by Tommy each fall after the frost had covered them a few times. This frost, I was told, was required to keep the pumpkins from rotting. The frost changed the composition of the pumpkin's innards.

Mr. Bergen had this theory that cows that were fed pumpkins were healthy cows. So Tommy had the honour of slicing the huge pumpkin in half or even quarters and placing these pieces on a pumpkin slicer machine. A huge contraption the pumpkin slicer was, the only one I have ever laid eyes on. One hand pushing the unwieldy pumpkin into the slicer, which had a 3-foot diameter-rotating wheel with sharp knifes on it. The other hand turned the crank that chopped up the edible gourd for the bovines to enjoy. The cows seemed to enjoy the treat, sort of like *Alpencruter* to Mr. Bergen I thought!

The long rows of watermelons were also picked just ahead of a serious frost, although the Bergen gardens had huge overhanging trees with loads of foliage that kept the fruits and veggies below from frost longer than most gardens. This extra growing time resulted in the melons being extra sweet, with the beets and potatoes so fully developed they almost walked on their own to the root cellar!

The melons were placed in salt brine, in huge wooden barrels with the metal straps belting the various rounds on the outside of the barrel. Large bunches of dill weed was also mixed into the brine, plus likely some secret other ingredients. Don't get me going on the *Alpencruter* thing! A lid that fit into the barrel was weighted down with football-sized rocks. Left to marinate for a few weeks or a few months, the melons absorbed the brine and, in this marinating process, even the rind turned edible or at least nice to suck on if you like a vinegar taste as I do! Was it Mr. Bergen or was it Anna, they were king of marinated melons in my mind. After Mr. Bergen did pass on, the answer was clear, it had been Mr. Bergen's secrets that were now missing in Anna's attempts to duplicate his melons but never matched her Dad's results.

So many times in winter when I delivered the mail to the Bergens, I came scampering over the hard snow drifts, back to our house with a sour melon wrapped in an old *Rundschau* newspaper.

Mr. Bergen seemed delighted by my short scampering legs on my return trip from his yard, the melon tucked under my arm like a football player headed for a touchdown!

Visiting the Bergen home was a rare treat. The furniture was all very old at that time. The dim lights from the oil lamp did little to boost optimism of sight or mind—but the Bergens were a friendly lot.

For toys, to keep me occupied, a large bottom drawer was pulled from the homemade chest of drawers.

Here were all shapes and sizes of dried gourds. The stems, like the rest of the dried garden species, were now petrified, first with the hearth oven, as well as the many years in the drawer. The seeds inside were hard, rattling about loosely inside the hardened veggie, ideal to jam in a band! By shaking several at a time, a rather delightful tune came about.

Also in the drawer were many wooden, crudely carved farm animals. Homemade wooden building blocks became houses and barns for the animals. While the mind was searching for new ideas, the dried gourds shook out a one-of-a-kind tune. Not that I would have cared to spend many nights on this assortment of entertainment, it served the purpose for the night and placed a wonderful memory in perpetuity!

Easily the most intriguing piece of furniture, or is it an appliance, was the hearth brick oven built into the house when it was constructed in the late 1800's or early 1900's. It is my understanding that the Bergens not only built the house and barn, but Mr. Bergen built this rather rare hearth oven himself.

The opening to the oven was with a large heavy metal door that swung on huge cast iron hinges. This oven door faced the kitchen and was about two feet square. The oven was some six to eight feet long or deep and stood six feet tall. This back part of the oven jutted totally into the living room. It had a rounded, half moon top. The finish on the hearth was a canvas type that could withstand the heat well.

The oven was used for baking but equally important, provided the heat for the entire house. Only in summer was the giant oven allowed to cool down and a regular cook stove in the kitchen was fired up for baking and cooking purposes. The top cast-iron metal door revealed a brick shelf baking chamber, where many pans of bread would be placed for baking at one time.

Just below was the fuel fire chamber door. The fire hearth was large and many manure wafers, plus coal or wood was placed for the enjoyment of the furious fires.

Where this rare hearth oven idea was taken from remains unclear to me, but a good guess would likely be from Russia.

The main fuel was the manure wafers that had an extra amount of straw mixed in for better and faster combustion.

On our farm we did have a similar hearth oven but ours was outside, near our summer kitchen. My recollection of this oven is limited, but I recall mom making waffles in it, as well as baking bread.

On a quiet, almost breezeless day, our yard was filled with the aroma of the whole wheat bread baking.

When mom did remove the bread, allowing it to cool a mite, the bread knife still had steam rising from the loaf as she was cutting the awaited slices!

Fresh hand-churned butter on a steaming slice, the butter sat in the bread pores like small ponds! To describe such a taste, words fail me!

Many a day, mom was able to make a light supper after the family had sat in the shade, near the fired up hearth, and enjoyed heaven on earth!

Unfortunately the weather had been unkind to the oven and it was dismantled rather than repaired!

On our farm we used horse sled to haul the manure into the pasture away from the house. Flies were a huge problem and a manure pile in the backyard attracted flies to the manure and then to your back door.

On many farms, cow manure was trucked out of the barns on a daily basis with a wheelbarrow into the area behind the barn, as it was on the Bergen farm. As the manure pile grew the wheelbarrow was pushed up the mucky sloops and dumped on a certain side of the pile. The best fuel was created with aged manure, so the new was not to be mixed with the aged side of the pile, ready to be "wafered" in late fall.

Come winter the track was frozen but very bumpy. One side of the compost pile was now allowed to dry & age. The more years of composting the better it seemed for the products use.

May be hard to believe, but the housewife had great input as to the make up of the manure pile!

Some housewives wanted more straw to be used in the barn, making the wafered fuel a quicker combustion in the oven fire chamber.

A "wafer machine" was brought in and, powered by a small engine, would take the hand-pitched manure from the hopper and compress the dung into wafers about a foot by a foot and six inches deep. Extra straw could be added at this point in the process, to custom make the fuel to the cook's liking. This "patty-cake" machine then shoved the formed wafers out the back, where human hands would make neat rows and piles of these wafers in fence like rows, so the wind could do its drying action. Year-long drying or more made the best fuel. These wafers were then tossed into the oven, furnace-hearth oven and burned cleanly without a smell and almost ash free. Each fall the "dry side" of the giant compost heap was compressed into wafers for the winter heating supply.

Some farmers were known to sell dung wafers to town folks that did not have a compost heap.

The wafers of course were also used in conjunction with fossil fuels such as coal and wood. The reason dung wafers burnt so well was the farmers generous use of straw for cow bedding, which of course ended in the manure gutter. Costs were kept to a minimum and burning manure wafers was a real recycling effort.

Tommy, who lived upstairs in the Bergen house, did confide to my siblings that despite layers of blankets he was frozen in the harshest winter nights, as the heat from the brick oven had to find its way upstairs in the drafty old building on a voluntary basis. Tommy was rarely permitted to have visitors, so his room remains a mystery to me except for Tommy's description.

Tommy was not a complainer and lived under the work for board arrangement for many years.

One sunny afternoon several cars did arrive at the Bergen farmyard in convoy fashion. From our farmyard we could hear a loud discussion taking place. When the cars left, Tommy was in one of them and the work arrangement had come to an end. We later learned that Tommy's brothers "had rescued" Tommy by his request from this arrangement.

Tommy kept touch with my folks and siblings from time to time. Tommy's dedication and work ethic had been recognized in the workplace and held a fine job, at last report, in the Toronto area.

The Bergen's farmyard heart had been wrenched from them when Tommy left. The Bergen's never complained, but the evidence was noted very early after Tommy left. Livestock was sold off to a bare few animals. Laying hens no longer cackled. The gardens fell into disrepair, one by one. Anna was a hard working gal, but the task was ominous. Mrs. Bergen became more frail and passed away on a cold winter day. As a young lad I was so saddened by her passing, but did learn that the world carries on, even if it did hurt.

Mr. Bergen pressed on but his body, too, was spent.

After Mrs. Bergen's passing, Mr. Bergen felt lonely and often came for a visit to our yard. He was not keen on big meals but

Mom knew Mr. Bergen enjoyed the coffee and something to go with it. As always, Mom complied with the perceived need in his life, as she served many a *faspa* (Mennonite coffee break) for him, regardless what time he arrived. His daughter "Iron Anna" was not a cook, which made Mr. miss his wife even more.

A few years later at our annual school picnic, Mr. Bergen was enjoying watching us play baseball. Sitting in the shade of our growing maple trees, he leaned backwards and, without a word, expired!

The picnic, by family request, did continue, but for me it was a bitter sweet event. The play was fun but a man I had known for so long and had learned from was now history! I shed a few tears as I saw his overall-bib-clad body being loaded into a hearse.

Anna however was undaunted, it seemed. In her higher thirties I suspect, but in fine fettle, she continued to bravely farm on.

Anna's personal life in fact got a boost of sorts, her first love!

Should I qualify that and say, first love that I know of? Anna was 30 years my senior, who was I to know what water had run under the bridge before I happened along!

Anna had shown no inclination that she craved a partner. Her parents now both departed and living entirely alone, she was financially secure. Anna had inherited the family homestead, a chunk of farmland she rented to others, the family car and some cash.

The new teacher at Fairfield, a single, good looking dude, same church as Anna, but "teacher had no car."

Therein lays the mystery; was it Anna, or was it the transportation that Mr. Buller was looking at?

As the folklore goes, a certain farmer put an ad in the lovelorn section of a newspaper, Wanted: women with tractor, please send picture of tractor.

The arrangement, while not clear to onlookers of which there were many, it also caused consternation in the Bergen heir group section. To the apparent heirs of Anna, it was somewhat disturbing! To Anna, it was love, she deserved some!

Mr. Buller, the school teacher, was about 12-15 years her junior, Anna was willing to overlook that fact, while Mr. Buller looked it over! Transportation was a big item to him, he was hitch hiking on weekends, yet a proud man—driving was really what he should be doing, his demeanor called for it! Champagne taste but beer income, they say! Anna seemed like "the ticket" for both of his dilemmas! Anna liked the attention and Mr. Buller, the transportation; the speculation carried on. The narrow, non-maintained, rutted road that ran between our farm and the Bergen's led past the school grounds, only 200 yards up that road, where Mr. Buller lived in the teacherage.

Anna was not a demanding type, just some attention seemed to fill her bill. Mr. Buller liked driving her car, which he did with Anna the passenger—always!

The car was bought new by Mr. Bergen right after the war ended, a mid-forties black Dodge four door sedan. Mr. Bergen had driven the car primarily to church and back, thus very low mileage and in mint condition.

On the lone prairie, where life can become rather "routine," any such late blooming love story will get the neighbourhood chins a-wagging and it did! On one occasion when some neighbour lady stuck the verbal pin in Anna, about the coming and going from the school yard, or better said the teacherage, Anna loudly laughed off the jibe by saying, "life begins at forty!" I now realized that Anna had more reading material than I had thought, as the German *Rundschau* weekly paper did not contain such modern quips. While *Rundschau* has a raunchy twang sounding name, it was anything but! It was a paper, my mom told me, of the comings and goings of people in the Mennonite spectrum, however it was not a "love lorn rag for the lonely"! At least the *Rundschau* want ads did not reflect such romantic requests, although it may have carried some *Alpencruter* ads!

The relationship for Anna appeared to be growing, for Mr. Buller, well, it was another trip!

The relationship "hit a bump on the road," quite literally, some time later.

That narrow road leading past the schoolyard and to Anna's farmyard was the beginning of the end. Mr. Buller knew how to run "a narrow line" in his personal (love) life but was not as adept at driving it!

It was an early summer night, school was still in session, when we noted from our yard, Mr. Buller trotting to Anna's house. It was church night and Mr. Buller was running a bit late.

The black Dodge roared to attention, when Mr. Buller hit the starter. Mr. Buller had a tendency to lay on the gas pedal rather hard and speed was his passion. The Dodge was by no means accustomed to such lead foot behaviour! Mr. Bergen and Anna both liked to idle the black baby a bit and then gently ease the car unto the road.

On this night in question the black Dodge heeded the command of Mr. Buller's lead foot. As they neared the schoolyard, the car unexplainably skidded sideways on a dry road, jumped the shallow ditch and mowed down several of the hefty wooden poles that held the checkered wire school fence.

The evening was in ruins! The Dodge, now much calmer, returned to the Bergen farmyard with a reshaped front fender and bumper. The pounding of heavy hammers was heard late into the night, as the battle between man and metal was fought. Seeing the car some time later, it appeared the metal had won!

Now the "chins" in the neighbourhood were wagging! All the school kids saw the damaged fence, Mr. Buller was not talking, but the kids were!

Why did the accident happen? Why did Mr. Buller lose control of the car? Was he momentarily distracted? If so, by what? Mr. Buller's passion for speed was noted by several. Another person had seen Anna and Mr. Buller driving only a few days before and felt Anna "had sat, well, near the center" of the front bench-style car seat. Had this occurred again and had this distracted the driver? As a twelve-year-old and it's your teacher that's messed up, you bet that's a story!

The open and unofficial inquiry went on for some time without ever arriving at a hard conclusion.

The summer holidays were upon all, which meant Mr. Buller would be spending his summer at his aging parents home.

When school resumed in fall, the saga of Anna and Mr. Buller—lets say the bloom was off the rose! Anna's car had taken a beating, and it seemed the romance had as well. Anna again was busy preparing what was left of her garden for the coming winter. The melon patch had shrunk greatly. The cows were now on a no pumpkin diet. The *Alpencruter* was gone for man & beast!

Anna, however, proved her mettle once more! While speculation had been rife that Anna might sell out her farm and take to town life, that was talk from others. Anna was a product of the land!

Living alone and taking on challenges that she ought not to caused us to be concerned if we noted lack of movement on Anna's yard.

One such time when we thought the action was lacking, I biked down the short lane to take a closer boo at the farm.

Anna appeared from the back of her farmyard with the standard grin in place, her dress however had met with a definite dirt pile! Anna had her favorite small dog on her arm. Seems the normally indoor dog had been let out and chased a stray cat under the large empty granary that was set on wooden blocks. With the uneven dirt under the building, the cat had made it under the floor joists and dirt, out the other side, but not her silly dog.

The dog was now stuck half way under the large building and it was whining. Anna too began to crawl, snake like under the granary floor, to rescue the pooch. The space narrowed, but fearless Anna crawled on till she too found herself stuck as well, about 3 feet from her beloved dog!

All morning she scratched and clawed with her bare hands, while being pinned by granary floor joist and dirt!

She thought of hollering, she told me, but knew she would not be heard. The thought of death had been but a fleeting thought. Yes the neighbours (us) would check on her if we saw no movement on the yard, she comforted herself with, if not today, then tomorrow. Her hands clawed some more and now the dog had managed to free herself and was licking Anna's face, she must not despair!

After several hours of "dogged" determination, she did free herself and wriggled out from under the death trap, butt first. Meeting her, she did look like a mole after a morning workout! Shaken? Not Anna, a change of clothes and she was ready to salvage what was left of the day.

She was however pleased that we had responded so quickly to what could have been a very serious incident.

Her house was much too large for her alone. Anna sealed off the upstairs to conserve heating. Finally she was confined in winter months to her kitchen, where she set up her bed as well. Anna no longer used the brick hearth oven.

Anna's farm was being overrun with weeds, which brought on the rodents and closely behind came the skunks; that follows the food chain of animals. Soon there were too many skunks and the overflow came to our farm.

Anna bravely fought the situation in some unorthodox manner. Anna would not touch a gun but she was a dead ringer with anything else she held in her hand. One day, when walking through some weeds, she came upon a skunk. Anna knew the spraying distance of a skunk. She threw the hammer at the skunk from about 15 feet away and nailed the poor critter— dead on one shot! Then next, while on the same path, she was with some metal snips in her hand. Metal snips are not an Olympics event toss to my knowledge, but Anna hit the skunk with one clunk, total skunk write-off!

Other instances she told me of and always the same result! By summer's end the score was Anna, ten, skunks, zero!

In later years after I left the area, Anna did sell the farm and move to town. Alzheimers took its toll on one very tough iron lady!

Anna Bergen, my iron lady and mentor

A Streetcar I Desired

A trip to the big, bad City of Winnipeg was an adventure of huge proportions in my growing up years. Very few kids, in fact it seemed I was the only kid my age to be able to describe the city landscape to my peers in grade one at Spears school. Oh yes, explain I did! I cannot recall not being able to answer a question, or recall any event that required my vast knowledge!

Dad knew but one route to Eaton's parking lot, that is, providing there were no mandated detours from construction and such. Eaton's was the department store of choice for our family. If time allowed or selection dictated, then a brisk walk into the cold wind (both ways) to the Hudson's Bay was made, aptly called "The Bay."

The Bay was always the "prettier store," considered "more expensive" I was told, but very fine selection. Even in those "way back days," ladies were concerned about wearing something they might meet on the street or, heaven forbid, at the next gathering or wedding!

The long escalator rides were a fascination to my little mind, actually still are today, just a bit more hidden I trust. Then the elevators, the sudden gulp on liftoff, the bouncy stop. All this caused by the human operator right in the elevator at that time. These operators rode the elevator all day, depositing shoppers on the correct floor, whatever they were looking for.

The operators came in all shapes, sizes and temperments, I found. A pygmy step of mine towards the control area of this machine of "mass destruction," could set off sound waves from the white-gloved, high strung operator! "The silly cage could at best go up or down, jeepers creepers lady," I thought, but Dad's hand was already on my shoulder, pulling me back. I gave Dad and the lady my Low German protest—feisty I could be too! Her gloved hand pulled the smooth running accordion type of grill gate aside in the elevator, then another one on the floor where we had arrived. Most operators, be they with either set of plumbing, would be pleasant and offer me a closer boo at the controls. Heck, I was offered to stand right next to a black lady, she put her arm with the white glove around my stocky shoulder and said, "Hey boy, you move the controls on the next one!" Well I had only but laid my virgin Mennonite eyes on a few black-skinned people for the first time, that day! But any lady, never mind skin colour, that puts her arm around me and allows me to run this here contraption that at the moment I felt controlled the world, an even up swap for my Granny right here and now!

I moved the lever with authority, the loaded cage moved down as she winked to the captive passengers. She announced the floor with her raspy Nat King Cole voice, and I reached for the caged door handle with my ungloved hand and pulled back. It slid like a hot knife through butter! Some of the passengers disembarked, with a few giving me a pinch as they went by, one gave a pat on my pumpkin shaped head! Oh if only I had brought my straw hat, that tall straw hat, those quarters would be flowing into my sweaty palm now! Dad saw I was having a "pinnacle" moment, and allowed our intended floor to slip by, as I handled a few more floors with my black lady's blessing!

What a difference from the previous shoo-shoo "bag" of a gal we had as an operator! "Oh, give me more black ladies," my little heart sang all day!

As we finally left the elevator, my "newly-traded-for black grandma," gave my short bod a hug. My face about hip height and I put my stubby arm, or tried to around her, err, butt, well better than half way, giving her a gentle hug! What's a guy to do? She had made my day, and she knew it!

I made up my mind right there and than, when I get to Heaven a few "hellos" to loved ones I will make! Then it's "Where is the black Granny I adopted in the Eaton's elevator when I was about yea high?" I will proceed to tell her what she meant to me in my lifetime, as I trudged the dusty old earth, as she did I am sure. If the line up of people wanting to Thank her is not too long, tea for two please, I just know she was a blessing to a throng of people!

With all this excitement, what does a young man need but an "outhouse"! Well in the City they have toilets, later that changed to washrooms, even lavatories in snooty company. Powder room for the fairer sex. Get this, back in the forties Eaton's had slots on the washroom doors! Oh yes, it cost you a nickel and no refunds should you find yourself constipated! Some "tight wads," I am told, sat there for hours, just insisting that they get their money's worth.

Then there were those who stood on the ready, when someone was leaving the washroom stall, quickly catch the door before it closed, a nickel saved is a nickel earned! But old ma' Eaton had that washroom cop making his rounds all day, if he caught you trying to save the nickel, (I with Dad did witness such an attempt), the burly cop would look over the top of the washroom door and insist on a nickel in cash. It worked, with some choice greetings exchanged that Dad said he could not clearly understand what was said! The washroom cop also had a good memory and certain men that had a bad track record of attempting to slip by without paying would be ushered out upon being spotted or paying the nickel to the cop, who then slotted the nickel for the slippery guy. PR was not a concern for Eaton's in the washroom. Although the cop was kind to us when questioned as to Dad and me going into the stall together, the nod was given. The flushing toilet was a first for me as well. What a waste of water, I thought! The toilet doors, about a foot off the floor, and sure enough some guys attempted to squeeze under the door. With a dozen stalls to watch, the cop missed the first part of his attempt to squeeze under the door but caught him with a sharp rap on the rump from the Cop's size twelve boot. The Cop put in a nickel, opened the door, said nothing, nor did the knock-kneed customer as he was leaving! To a young wide-eyed country boy, this was quite an education!

The streetcar ride Dad had promised, well I was almost ready to forgo it, my little brain was racing and desperately afraid if I added any more adventure into this round pumpkin head called a brain, something would be squeezed out and forgotten! I could not spare a memory from today!

I could not however disappoint Dad, even a bit! Streetcars were something Dad had talked to me about for several years or, in my young mind, a long time before this trip. We stood on the sidewalk in front of the giant Eaton's building, that huge, how many storey building Dad? We rode all the way to the top Dad? Could I ride with "the black lady" (scwattia fru) in the elevator all the way up and down again? Dad realized my mind was not over the last adventure yet. Dad looked at his watch. Maybe we should wait for Mom "under the clock" in Eaton's. Dad wanted my full attention when riding the streetcar, without any elevator questions; best to have lunch first.

Meeting under the Eaton's clock had become a "Mennonite hang out"! Throughout the city and stores, the English tongue prevailed. Oh yes, in the *"Nort ent"* (North End) one could be forgiven in thinking that the Tower of Babylon was being re-enacted judging by the different tongues spoken, otherwise it's English throughout Winnipeg. Under the Eaton's clock, its *Platt Duetch* or Low German, Mennonite, spoken here!

On such a rare trip to the city, Mom and the sisses liked to split from us grubby men. The women loved to browse the "delicate section," where slinky, see-through items were sold by the D cup and such. Man wanted the area where items were also stacked, but sold by the gallon! So a time was agreed upon, the meeting place under the Eaton's clock of course!

So it was a ten minute wait for the other party (if you were lucky), brought about a good deal of info about the others waiting. The clock itself was hanging from the ten-foot ceiling, a four-sided job, with large, "Uncle Ben" type numbers. The wooden framework made it look like you should really obey and be on time. It seemed to have this effect only on the men, the women's arrival ten to thirty minutes late was always due to a misunderstanding, always the men's fault, thus the lunchtime mood began.

Lunchtime at Eaton's, for the Mennonites, was an escapade to behold, or best, remember!

I actually enjoyed the undertaking! Eaton's at that time had a huge grocery department and were very modern compared to the hunt-grab with a stick and claw, the staff used at Gladstone in Winkler when corralling an errant box of corn flakes. Eaton's mass displays of toilet paper and such made my eyes bug out! What did the city folk do with their old Eaton's catalogues I wondered as I pondered another toilet paper display! Big wire baskets on wheels, people pushing them, just taking stuff from the open long shelves! Were they stealing stuff?

Eaton's also had the latest in the restaurant! Cafe-style-eatery thingy, it was called a cafeteria. "Calf," to this farm lad, was something a cow had each spring! With no command of the English language at this point in life, my folks marginally better, some word pronunciations were a riot I feel certain. Mom was always embarrassed, Dad never! Cafe, Dad pronounced as "cavf." A hamburger sounded more like "burglar" than burger, but he never went hungry, so it was working he said!

The plates, bowls and cutlery came first, after you picked up a large flat tray. Now you slide the tray along the thigh high shelf provided and make your selection from the foods provided over the side. This could take some getting used to. Where are the prices? A Mennonite has a tough enough time with a menu and the prices given. Mennonites read the menu starting at the right-hand side, "Ah yes, here is something, sixty-five cents, yes—yes hamburger steak! If it comes with soup, coffee and dessert, you got a deal!"

"The soup is no longer included? Two hamburger steaks then, (kids can have a bit of mine) one soup, we can share! Hot water please, ketchup is free, this helps the soup along a bit!"

We watched one guy—yes, he was greasy looking, a street guy no doubt. He ordered hot water, snuck an empty soup bowl, poured the hot water in, half a bottle of ketchup later, perhaps a dozen crackers, all compliments of Mr. Eaton! His lunch was complete! The waitress said, "Every day!" Dad felt the nickel at the washroom was a bit of a trade off for the free soup.

The lunch was a rush job if we wanted to hit up The Bay today, which we did. Mom and Sis's wanted to window shop, so Dad and me took the streetcar. Time and the huge lunch of tidbits of ground beef, the crackers were there for the taking, chocolate bars were a nickel, all this had settled me down from my high of the elevator ride, plus the mental adoption of my black granny! Now I was ready to concentrate on the streetcar ride and do justice to Dad's highlight of the day.

The banging-clanging of the streetcar wheels as they clicked along their embedded tracks in the pavement was a marvel to behold. The long arms that protruded from the roof of the bus seemed to have no visible reason to stay way up there. I was told these long arms gave the streetcar the electric power to run along its tracks. I accepted the answer and moved my mind to other things that hopefully I could grasp!

Electric power! We could only dream of such a luxury for our little farm. We watched the traffic lights change, one side of the traffic came to a squeaking halt while the other street was speeding across the minutes ago *verboten* intersection. The cars we were seeing were, for the most part, much newer and sleeker looking than what our farm kin were tooling about the countryside.

Some cars had a sign on it that read "Taxi." Dad explained that these were cars that were available for you to rent complete with driver. This thought of cost just baffled my mental bank capacity to comprehend such funds to lay waste to. To question such "waste" as I saw it would most likely be explained by the adults that *"the Englanda"* (the Englishman) has that kind of money. So for many of my growing up years, if the person had only the "English tongue," then he was an *Englanda* and rich! That myth, as so many others, was proven incorrect in years to come. For now that was fine, taxis were for the rich only.

Finally Dad felt the watching of the streetcars had run its course, it was time to participate. We stood in line and far too soon, as I was assessing the world from my three feet high vantage point, it was our turn to step onto the noisy street car that came to rest in front of us.

The conductor opened the doors with such dignity, I felt sure I would mess this trip up with my country habits. The streetcar was packed with people, it was standing room only. The conductor seemed to take his position very seriously and announced the next stop, as if he were introducing a star player at the seventh game! To me, it was preposterous that a grown man should be on a streetcar all day, shouting out street names, go home and claim a days work! Gosh, only a farmer, hauling hay, slopping the pigs, that was a day's work! Not this sissy streetcar stuff! Certainly he would soon get a real job!

The streetcar driver stood as I recall and did his clang-clang, bang-bang thing with the few levers he had to work with, making them seem overly important I felt. It was electric, no gears to shift! No steering wheel, it was on steel tracks like a train! It appeared he took out some frustration on people on bicycles and some cars as he needlessly rang the bell on the streetcar with his foot! He seemed to expect it would make a difference or elevate his importance as streetcar driver, feed his ego at best!

The streetcar doors opened, front, mid and back, where another conductor did his shtick to draw a paycheque as well. They did it with a straight face! "Do they really get paid for this?" I asked Dad. Dad assured me they did and it was a tougher job than it looked; Dad was being a wimp, I thought, but I moved on with my thoughts.

Men gave up their seat for ladies, please and thank-you' filled the air. The driver ran his fingers along his handle bar mustache, just to be sure no unnoticed air turbulence had wrecked havoc with his prize since he checked it a block ago! His skycap too was checked in the mirror to be sure the ladies had noticed the cocky position he had given the cap on his graying noggin! Next stop, he took out a special soft cloth he had tucked away from the public eyes view and ran it gently across his well-polished shoes. These were his work shoes; boy, he should see my dad's farm workboots!

Overhead on each side of the streetcar ran a clothesline looking cord. Passengers seemed to take turns giving the cord a tug, yet no immediate action resulted, perhaps a lone ting of a bell could be heard.

Dad said this indicated to the driver that they wanted to disembark at the next stop. "But why did five or ten people pull the cord when one would do?" I thought. City folks!

The streetcar came to a grinding halt in the middle of the street. The bus went dark, no one had pulled the cord! Dad explained that the long stick, that I felt had no good reason to stick up on the roof of the bus to draw the power, had finally done what I felt it should have done a long time ago, just dropped dead! Justice was finally served, I felt as I sat there smugly, the only passenger to know this had to happen, it was this country lad thing!

The driver put on some oily looking gloves and left the bus. One could tell this was really much below his dignity, and those stinky gloves and his fine manicured mustache just did not belong in the same picture. The lights came on, the gloves off, the bus again leaped into action and soon we were at the Bay.

Dad explained that the long wand that stayed up for no good reason that I could see had jumped off the overhead electric wires. The bus driver had now re-connected the long wand, which was spring loaded to keep it up to the wires.

Yes, the Bay was a very snazzy looking store! All those marble floors and pillars! The escalators were longer, more fun to ride than Eaton's too! But the elevators were not. The operators of the elevators seemed to be bothered by a young lad's probing fingers and smiling face. I was soon ready to return to the comforts of Eaton's. Eaton's, I was convinced, understood a young lad! The walk back to Eaton's, about the distance of walking to my Spears school, but much more exciting—even dangerous. The cars seemed—better said the car drivers were reckless compared to the careful drivers I was accustomed to in our little country towns. Pedestrians in the city were only a bother, it seemed. By day's end, I longed for the serene countryside again.

The ride home was considerably shorter, at least the part I can remember! The excitement had taken its toll on my body, I had nodded off before we left the city throngs! It did however require several recesses and lunch hours to relay all the excitement to my classmates at Spears.

The Sommerfelders

This church was an example of spartan Mennonite lifestyles! There were and are churches in southern Manitoba that had similar spartan worship houses much beyond my growing up years.

I am not judging right or wrong; its just that, in today's world, to see such a basic house of worship is unique. Also, having attended this church in my early youth has special significance.

In the forties, when my parents attended the Sommerfelder Church, it was already then noted for its simplicity—much remains the same. The horse hitching rails are gone, the vehicles the worshippers arrive in are much sleeker, the colours are now a rainbow compared to the consistent black we saw back when.

The building itself however is much the same. Yes, there have been breakaway splinter groups or, in a kinder term, "sister churches" established, but the core group is still stuck in the past. Again, neither right nor wrong, the cars in the parking lot versus the buildings are a stark contrast!

The Old Colony Mennonite Churches also have remained "as we had it," a common Mennonite refrain. Ministers then and now are largely unpaid servants of the Lord. Many are farmers, some businessmen, some common labour, but all committed to the Gospel and the shepherding of their flocks.

Elders and Deacons are elected, generally a life term. Ministers again, are "called by God," then affirmed by the membership, also for life.

Back in my days, some today, did not approve of the use of hydro in the Church, although they fully availed themselves of the "English Power," the moniker the hydro carried in its early days in the Mennonite community, in their homes. Some churches did permit use of hydro in the basement for lighting and the much handier way of preparing foods and storing it in electric fridges. Inconsistency in thoughts or practices did not have to be explained or justified then or today it would seem.

One Old Colony worshipper shared his feelings on the hydro issue with these thoughts: "It is not that we are against the use of hydro for our business, and even Church basement events. We do not have hydro in our home as a constant reminder that, according to Scripture, we are not to be a 'part of the world, only in the world'! Hydro in the home encourages us or makes it easy to have a radio, TV etc. By denying ourselves of hydro in the home, these temptations are not a problem." I had to respect that, it was and is their right to practice this lifestyle, and certainly does have merit if you can sell this to your family, while all around you, the kids are exposed to the real world speeding by.

The Elders of the church had enormous powers over the congregations. In many cases it was only after a long serving Elder or Pastor passed away that a fresh approach could be openly considered, perhaps implemented, on new practices in the church. The dogma of the past was the dogma of today, likely tomorrow as well.

Musical instruments were complete taboo in the church and that included pianos and organs. Privately I knew of and heard some of the church members sing and play a variety of musical instruments. A beautiful job they did, but in private settings, not in the framework of the white walls, the slatted-park style benches of the Sommerfelder Church.

The "lead" singers in the Sommerfelder Church were an act to behold in the church service! A direct translation from the Low German would be *"fore singers"* or lead singers, and lead they did!

The buildings all had much the same appearance; you have seen one, then you have seen all!

They were a one storey wood structure, most times a basement for eating purposes. The entrances were always a standard welcome, of wood porches that were well-coated in gray paint. Windows were the basic "push me up type" if you were warm, worshippers did so to suit their own liking. The walls, a stark white with no pictures, the benches either painted white, brown or heavily varnished, so as to avoid getting a splinter in no-no land!

The front, or pulpit-end area, had a raised platform the entire width of the church building.

In the middle was a tall wooden pulpit, wrap around, somewhat like the bow of a ship. It was horseshoe shaped, tall and near the top the pulpit jutted out at an angle, again, like a boat that plowed water. So the total black dressed Pastor, stepped behind or into this large, generally white pulpit, his arms could now rest on the adequate sides, while the front was sloped upwards, making a six foot man seem rather modest, perhaps only from breast pocket up showing the Worshippers! To each side of the pulpit were the "singers" benches, with a "flower planter rail," less the flowers, in front of the singers only. A few steps on either side of the pulpit allowed access for the Minister as well as the coveted singers.

In the very back was a modest size room on either side of the entry, they were called *"stavkes,"* meaning a quiet or baby room, although few babies were ever brought to church that I saw.

The men's side *"stavke"* was used as a meeting place for the Minister of the day, plus the "fore singers."

A very high white ceiling throughout the building gave much-needed air space, as various fragrances from the different families (house and barn combined) were mingled at such a gathering. Soap and water was all you had to ward off perspiration odours! In some cases the soap either failed or the bathtub must have sprung a leak! These cases fortunately were rare, but it seemed "strongly" represented in those rare situations. White gumdrops, spearmint, was the only flavour to fight bad breath with or to hold your taste buds at bay.

Women wore the big black headdresses, kerchiefs or shawls perhaps, which most times had some fancy embroidery on it in bright yellows and reds with some more modest oranges for background. The embroidery on the edges was a work of art! The dresses were ankle length, revealing just a bit of black stocking and dare I say leg! Fancy dress aprons were oft' worn over the all black dresses. The aprons often showed some colours. The shoes, some were high button, but most had the "modern, low-slung look" with only a single button closure.

No lipstick, earrings or necklaces! Hairstyles, of what was shown, were neatly combed. All wore at least shoulder-length hair, or would have been had the hair not been wound into a round ball at the back of the head. They were referred to as *"shups,"* in Low German, "push" or bun in English.

The front of the all black dresses were generous in size, even the bosom was left to your imagination! But, in some cases, the dress had no room for wrinkles and was "full house!" The "bra," while well displayed in the Eaton's catalogue (as an eight-year-old you keep tab on the trends), had not yet caught a foothold in all homes or persons, the result was a fair bit of action when the woman walked! Others simply said that these ladies were not "a breast" of the times!

Most of the women, though not all, were unconcerned about calories! In fact "that word" (calorie) had not reached the hinterlands of Mennonite country at that time. So to put it in perspective, a visual if you wish, a lot of ladies had "a nice welcome up front and an ample back porch as well!" The smile on their faces was radiant!

The men were in all black as well, at least most were. No neckties, but a shirt buttoned right to the top. Hey, that style is back! To think that a today's Sommerfelder member would be talked of "as cool and trendy," who would have thought it! Shoes were above ankle, well polished and laced. Headgear was left at the entrance area of the church, were for the most part a heavy, black tweed type.

One "howdy-do" type of bachelor came sauntering into the church service a tad late (big no-no), had his favorite heavyset tweed cap planted firmly on his sleepy noggin. An alert Deacon spotted the infraction, hastily snuck up to the offender (everyone saw it, including the Minister), and gently placed a tug on the offending head mat. The sleepy bachelor removed it slowly, brushed his uncombed hair with his five fingers and took in the service without flinching. Easy to see why he was single!

The men "carried" the wife's cooking rather well! Yes a few portly ones, but I can only gather the hard labour these farm folk did burnt off a lot of the calories they consumed!

Now with men and women firmly separated in the seating arrangement, where does that leave a young lad who might miss Mom and yet should weigh in on the men side? With latitude and possibly grace, I was permitted to choose in my very early days. After about age five, it was sitting with Dad, "After all you do want to be a man, don't you?" statement scurried me to the correct gender side!

Coughing seemed like a major problem to many. Hankies for the ladies helped but for the men it was the red bandana type, at times a good, loud snort was heard. Spearmint drops were quickly dispensed by a benevolent soul down wind from her or him, the coughing was generally cured.

A typical Sunday morning Worship service began at 8:30 a.m. Most of the worshippers arrived a half-hour early, with visitation the attraction. The entire congregation was abuzz till the singers and minister walked down the aisle, a hush of respect set in.

Men and women sat left and right on each side of the church, very definitely divided. The reasoning for this separation of husband and wife is another example of unexplained Mennonite mystery! All sat on park-like, slatted wood benches, no cushions. Most were farmers and the wood benches felt a lot softer to their rump than the binder or tractor seats, which were solid cold steel at that time.

My young, quick eyes noted some errant glances between the men and women sides. It was great drama on the way home from church, when Mom would make a statement that so and so lady had left the service twice, for a bathroom visit or whatever. Dad smelled a trick question, had not noticed a thing! Dad than made mention the certain gentlemen that had walked the aisle. Dad was certain it was for a smoke break outside, here again Mom (whose eyes missed not a peep) had not noted the male trip Dad spoke of!

I called it a draw!

The congregation in full buzz fell into an instant hush as the three to six singers (all male of course), minister in tow, made their way down the well painted, rugless, gray wooden floor to the front of the sanctuary. The minister wore a long, black jacket-overcoat combo with tails, which could be likened to a tuxedo.

One singer, after clearing his throat rather loudly, would name a page from the thick black songbook that had no notes, only words. A few moments pause, the page number again announced, the singer that named the song broke out in full voice! That notes were not required became apparent after the opening stanza! I can only trust that God's statement in the Old Testament carried forward into the New Testament, where it says "to make a joyful noise unto the Lord!" There was no piano or organ to cloak the screeches and the croaks, but the singers sang with gusto! The same could not be said for the congregation, but I, at times, felt that the singers did not mind, since this gave them a better chance to showcase their "operatic" singing voices! At times to me, it reminded me of a rusty door hinge! The verses were many! Another two to three songs were announced, right after the other song had died down. On one song, I saw the verses as twenty-seven! Each song by another singer, again the start was the same. I am sure there were some good voices in the group but many would have shattered any lead crystal had it been in the building!

The singing complete, the minister approached the pulpit in a solemn manner. Opened his well-worn scribbler, glanced over his flock. That was often the only eye contact the minister did make with the congregation during the entire presentation.

The minister read from his scribbler, word for word, a message he had given somewhere prior, sometimes oft before! These were travelling ministers and had no home church as such. Most ministers kept a little black diary, noting where and when a sermon had been given from which page. Not all ministers did so and it could happen, with a forgetful mind, a re-run of a sermon did occur! In a book on the history of Mennonite ministers, one minister had noted that he had given the same message seventeen times, hopefully at different churches!

The message was given in the Low German dialect. But for an unexplained reason, the call to prayer was given in the High

German language. At this point, the entire congregation turned and kneeled on the wooden floor, with elbows on bench, supporting the worshipping forehead. This call to prayer occurred twice for sure in every service, at times more. These prayer calls proved testy times for some. Many, mostly men, had dozed off as graciously as they could, hoping not to be noticed. Dad beside me too had his struggles with nodding off during the service, when the minister droned on in his total monotone voice, during his hour-long message.

Being a youngster, I looked around as to how many men were "snoozing." My counting was in its beginning stages, thus I found my count more accurate when I would point my tiny digit, or at least move my lips to keep up with my count. Dad, "worshipping with his eyes closed," had not noted my method of recording the others that were sleeping, some you could hear!

But no sooner had I exhaled that another service was behind me, as our car left the parking lot and the rest of the Sunday held promise than Mom lit into me in the car! Pointing at me, she explained with some emphasis that pointing was not nice, in church only I gathered! Certainly in the car it must have been fine, since she even wagged her finger to keep my attention. But I am ahead of myself.

Back in church, some were on alert, tapping the "sleepy guy" beside him whenever the minister's call to prayer came. This allowed him to take part in all phases of the service. The minister was very sincere and the message likely based on strong Biblical facts; it was the delivery of this message that just, well, made you sleepy! One Sunday, when the worshipper was missing his alert buddy who tapped his knee when the prayer call came, he was busted! The prayer call came, but not the knee tap! All of the congregation turned to kneel for prayer, except one! Since prayer in the Sommerfelder church was a personal, quiet process, the entire church was silent, even the kneeling minister. Silence, except for the lonely buddy's snores! The snore could now be heard throughout the church building! After the two minute prayer was finished, a sympathetic brother sat down beside the "sleepy" guy! When the next prayer call came, the tap on the knee did too; now he was in total harmony with the rest!

Messages could, and did, vary greatly in length. With an 8:30 start, the service could be done at 9:30 or it could also be 10:30. On occasion, I felt some of the minister's pages in the scribbler had stuck together and this shortened the sermon! Such variances spelt trouble for ardent smokers in the congregation. Some men walked out, doing what a puffer has to do, but not return to the service. I had a count on those as well! But one of the singers on the front perch, fore singers, well, he had a real problem too! A well-know chain-smoker, he would leave the service, walk the lonely aisle to the outdoors biff. Bladder problems were the official reason given, but most turned and smirked when he explained his exit then re-entry to the service. The poor boy had to lead the final song, after the minister would finally sign off. On rare occasion, a "short-winded" minister would catch him outside smoking, and another singer had to hastily improvise!

Now there were many times where the ministers seemed to not have communicated with each other (no phones), with no minister showing up for the service. The congregation then sang several songs and left for home, which meant about a half-hour total service. Rarely did this happen when I was compelled to go to church!

I counted the nail heads in the ceiling panels many times during the monotone service! Not actually panels but strips of narrow wood made the ceiling look like panels. Panels would have been modern, likely not allowed. I now practiced my nail head counting, with my hands below Mom's eye line! Even seated twenty-five feet away, and in a men's area that she never looked to, she knew precisely what I had or had not done!

I for one just had a terrible time with my "deposits and withdrawal" in the parents behaviour bank. I could do my best all week, gather the eggs, pull the weeds, slop the pigs, all that I felt was a pretty heavy deposit in the privately-owned behaviour bank my parents had. Come the weekend, I attempt to make a withdrawal, such as missing church, alas, the printout read, "not sufficient funds," at least according to the folk's record keeping. "How can that be?" I asked myself. Either the interest rate is high, calculated incorrectly, or my deposits are credited to my brother's account! I tried the overdraft protection route, Dad seemed to have some room there, but good ol' Mom, she ran things like a banker should, turn him down and debit his account for showing such audacity to ask!

I attempted many things to be able to stay at home from the Sommerfelder Church. The church may well have "fed" the spiritual needs of many, but not a kid of six to eight years old. I had instant tummy aches; you know, the kind that just kick in, doubles you over, but seems to subside when you see the tail lights of the folk's car down the driveway, on their way to church, without you! Oh bliss!

To my rescue came our neighbour lady, Anna Bergen. Anna was a Mennonite Brethren Church member (MB). The MB Church service did not commence till 11:00 a.m. This gave the kindhearted Anna a chance to conduct a small Sunday school class in the Spears school building. Sunday school began, lucky me, at 8:30 a.m. and was I enthused to go!

I was so excited all week about the new lessons to come that Mom and Dad, while they may have seen my motive, I was much to enthused to be turned down. "Regretfully," I would have to miss the Sommerfelder Church ordeal! An hour of Anna telling us about Jesus and I was free to go, ah sweet bliss!

Than there were times when Anna announced the week before, that next Sunday would not suit her for Sunday school, we had a week off. I may have "failed" to mention this at home! When next Sunday my folks roared off the yard for church, while I roared off into the wild yonder with my slingshot and collie Pup with me!

"What a way to enjoy God's creation," I thought! I rarely hit a bird with my slingshot. Pup caught no gophers for me, but the chokecherries in that far bush in the pasture were now ripe and tart. Pup relaxed as I climbed the tree and had a fill on the ruby red bunches of cherries. The cherries could however give one real stomach cramps, no acting required! They were called chokecherries for a good reason. I explained to Pup that I had some private matters to attend to and he took it well. Behind the large dead stump I dropped the overalls and fertilized that stump like it had never before known! It shot out new sprouts next spring!

My siblings thought I might have cut Sunday school a tad short, when I returned a bit too early. I had no timepiece on me, but they were satisfied with my explanation that Anna had to leave early. Sure I attempted to be honest, but I guess I ran my "honesty bank" along the same principles as the folks ran my behavioral bank account!

Almost got into trouble with this system but every system has its flaws. Again, Anna could not make Sunday school this Sunday. History repeats itself, and I "failed" to mention this at home. All went to church that day, except for me who was to attend Sunday school.

When our sedan shook up some dust as it left, Pup and myself headed for the vacated Bergen yard. I always made sure I had the details as to who would be attending their church. When she said she and her folks were going, my coast was clear. Pup was beside me, as we steered around the Bergen farmyard. The garden was showing signs of becoming neglected. Into the far gardens we went, where it was a pure bird menagerie. Sure I plunked a bird or two on its backside with my weak rubber slingshot, but no damage was done. I seemed to impress Pup with my accurate aim. We mucked about, did no harm but enjoyed the many large veggies growing. I was going to listen for the noise of our green sedan coming down the road, take the back route home, "Bob's your uncle!"

Hearing the roar of a car coming, I hardly took note till it turned into our driveway! How could they possibly be home so soon? I took the long way 'round to our house, approaching from the harmless dugout side of the farm. The abbreviated Sunday School story was bought once again! I discovered that the minister had been a no-show at the Sommerfelder Church, thus the early return. Pup just yawned as I told of the frogs in the dugout. The Sommerfelder Church had me beat, whether I attended or not!

Many churches, including the Sommerfelder, have made considerable changes in their worship services in the last years. Many congregations now have music to accompany the singing. Some, I understand, are still unchanged from the time of my youth. My focus in this book was to recall the past as I experienced it.

Teacher or Preacher?

For a youngster like me, being enrolled to begin classes in public school was exciting. Going to school meant you were growing up. Growing up seemed my mission and goal every morning, knowing I was one day older, one day closer to the magic, carefree world of being an adult! Adults made the rules that so governed my actions today! Adults decided the menu of the day! Adults could decide what work they would perform or take in that day! Adults, it seemed, did just as they pleased, at least from an about the three foot high vantage point that I viewed the world from! Adults could decide what clothes to wear, whether to hang up their clothes or drape them on a chair! This freedom was not in my grasp today! The adult world is what I longed for!

As a young lad, my choices were so limited, always subject to being corrected, changed—or worse, vetoed! Every day dreams I had of having "a perfect day" were often dashed by adults! Adults that had long ago forgotten what a perfect day could be like! In fact, by the blatant manner my dreams were thwarted on a regular basis, I questioned—in my mind only—if they had ever had a dream of their own!

So, the commencement of school attendance was a huge step towards the adult world that soon would be mine! Jumping through a few more hoops, like more grueling-boring days at school with subjects decided by adults but supposedly for kids!

School had the potential for being a great place to be, had it not been for the adult teachers! Learning was fun; the millions of questions I had floating in my fertile mind could be answered had not the fixed curriculum gotten in the way of such progress!

Books were a valuable source of info but most books, at least the ones that had the answers I required, were beyond my reading level. Verbal knowledge was fine with me, not having to do all the detail work before the desired info was imparted to me, via time-consuming tests and proper grammar! One teacher allowed open periods, and questions of all kinds could be asked. The teacher giving instant answers, allowing me to ask why, where, how, and when! These were the times I excelled! These were the days when all that knowledge would just flow from my prolific brain in torrents, like the flood waters in spring! Sadly though, these types of sessions did not show up on my report card!

While math and spelling became early favourites, I was interested in all facets of life, but not necessarily school subjects. Subjects are restricting, focussed, have restricting boundaries, which stunted the learning of new ideas on a wide vanguard. Subjects were the products of adults, most "adults" ran counter to my version of open learning.

Learning for me was sneaking away with my collie dog Pup. Laying in a sheltered gully, eating a self-made Dagwood sandwich, soda pop, looking at the open blue sky. The clouds would float by, some just narrowly missing the sun, some covering the sun, then watching the shade from the cloud racing across a field of grain. The sparrows and blackbirds were darting in, around, back again to their carefree feeding. The cloud now past caused the sunshine to race quickly to replace the fleeting shade. Ah, those clouds, so willowy, so soft, the many shape and sizes. Best of all, the clouds could not be changed by adults! Trees can be chopped down, the landscape changed in appearance by adults. The clouds were of God, the perfect creator, under perfect control!

I unwrapped the "Dagwood" sandwich, on this occasion consisting of jam, peanut butter, syrup with a thick slice of Dad's home-cured smoked ham, adhering to Mom's fresh baked bread. This was heaven or at least floating on a cloud! Best yet was that I had scarfed this monstrosity without leaving any tell-tale "skid marks" in the kitchen, the perfect heist!

A Dagwood sandwich could not be made for me by anyone else, at least according to my specs! A Dagwood was a personal creation that could vary according to one's mood, but largely effected by the ingredients on hand at the time in our well-stocked pantry. It was a melding of fine ingredients that only a young mind could muster up and amalgamate into one feast! To request such a combination in a sandwich from an adult would be met with a volley of objections. It might be too rich, it might be too much, with no explanation of the meaning of "too much!" Dagwood, after all, was a cartoon character of the day, with his legendary sandwiches over a half foot high! The way Dagwood built his sandwich could not be done when his cartoon wife Blondie was near! The grin on Dagwood's face as he carried his prized work to a safe spot to consume was satisfaction in the making! The length I was compelled to go to, to make my own version of his efforts, was brutal!

The only option, whenever this young explorer was to go on a trek or fact-finding mission, was to prepare such a gourmet sandwich on your own, by yourself! One glance at my creation from Mom or sisters and the project was scuttled or suffered severe cutbacks!

Pup, being the true friend he was, could be trusted to maintain such a clandestine sandwich and menu secret, whenever I was able to construct a Dagwood creation, without disturbance from other stale minds! Sharing the sandwich with Pup assured the code of silence!

This was learning to me! A crow building its nest, noting the material it required. A gopher carelessly revealing where he lived. In the distance, the hot vapour from the sunshine rippling along in its endless quest for a destination. These were learning experiences!

A sharp rap on the desk from a heavy wooden ruler could only come from an adult teacher, reminding me that I was now attending a class. My yesterday's insightful thoughts once again spurned in favour of the drivel that the teacher's mind had decided to inflict upon me from his Dick and Jane type manual! This romantic novel about Dick and Jane told us that Jane was a girl and Dick was a boy! Such insights! Had the teacher, providing he knew, titillated the class with the anatomical differences of Dick and Jane, the teacher would have had my rapt attention through out the entire subject time allotted! These facts of life was what a lad seeks at a time in life where one languishes in true knowledge about the birds and bees!

The stork myth some time ago had been discredited by adults themselves with their flippant talk and behaviour about the "stork being due." The true facts of sex are not talked about that openly in Mennonite circles! Even a youngster caught onto that charade. Truth about sex came in whispers, winks, raised eye brows or quick glances to the younger set to be sure they are not catching on to the true facts!

Sure the Eaton's catalogue provided some clues, supplying fodder for the next recess, when young lads would discuss any new information that might have been gleaned since we last met and discussed such matters, likely the day before!

The mating of farm animals that our parents, despite best efforts, had not been able to shield our prying eyes from, was the best base of facts we had to work from. The process I described in detail, as I had witnessed our pigs mating the day before, was indeed fascinating, even revealing—the teacher's ruler again made harsh contact with his desk. His assumption was that he did not have everyone's full attention, not wishing to repeat himself. I, for one, was hoping he would not! Whatever he was attempting to describe was yesterday; I was interested in tomorrow!

After an energetic recess, it was time for my favorite subject, mathematics, today simply called math. In math there was accuracy! No teacher's leanings or opinions! No half-baked answers! There was even a master answer book where one could double-check one's result to a given problem. "Teacher's pets" had to operate at the same level as the rest did!

In math, you either had or you had not been correct. Adding, subtracting and multiplying was the few areas of life where you did not get concerned about who is giving you what information! What bias the teacher chose to apply to favour his "pets"!

Whether your current teacher was from the MB Conference or another conference, the answers were the same, all the students' answers were either right or wrong! In most other subjects, teacher's mild or strong bias was often present. In math whether you were Mennonite, Mark or Mary, two plus two was four!

Since the MB (Mennonite Brethren Conference) teacher in Spears school district chose to make an issue of which church or conference you attended, the mode of baptism, within the framework of school hours, it became a school issue! Allow me to digress, attempting to lay the groundwork for this contentious issue of local MB views on baptism, how they were expressed, affected or at times were inflicted on students in Spears school.

Before and during the writing of this chapter, I invested time to pray and meditate. I sought God's direction to my peace of mind that despite the various views that no doubt many students that attended Spears grade school may have, these are my experiences, my views, as I lived with them, saw them unfold, how they impacted me, likely others as well. The "misguided views," as I call them, that the MB teacher exposed, did affect many people lives living in that area and era.

Here is my take in a nutshell. While Mennonites attended many different churches with degrees of variation in practices but basically all having the same foundation of salvation in Jesus Christ. The different Mennonite churches have been compared to the various makes and models of automobiles. A different feature or look here or there, but in the final analysis, all take you to the same destination!

The conflict that caused ire in Spears school district was referred to as the Mennonite Brethren (MB) versus the General Conference (GC), the latter deemed all other than MB. The MB church practiced immersion in baptism, as they do today. The GC (or all others) practiced baptism by "pouring or sprinkling" in baptism, as they do today. The GC churches however recognized and accepted members that had been immersed by MB practices with full rights as church members when they decided to join. But, the local MB church did not accept members who had not been immersed. To fully join the local MB church you were compelled to be baptized again by immersion! Therein lay the crux of the matter! Young people were led through strife over this matter, before even married. Some young people in love decided to go there separate ways, when the baptism views could not be resolved. Often the young couple's parents were the catalysts in this problem. The parents became involved, which rarely solved the conflict. The GC parents standing firm that "one baptism" is what Scripture calls for, the pouring their offspring had undertaken was valid for life. The local MB view was that such a pouring was not valid and that in order to join the local MB church another baptism must occur, namely immersion.

I refer to "the local MB Church" at that time in my life. Later we were to discover that the MB churches in some other areas had always accepted and respected other forms of adult baptism. Full membership was possible without another baptism. In these "other" areas the conflict between GC and MB churches over baptism did not exist, thus little, if any friction, between MB and GC existed.

The official MB position on baptism is and has been as follows: I quote from the *MB Herald Article 8. Practice*—"We practice water baptism by immersion administered by the local church. Local congregations may receive into membership those who have been baptized by another mode on their confession of faith." End of quote. Where then did this discrepancy arise in the Spears and Flatfields area?

In my childhood it appeared to be a few MB families that held strong leadership positions in the local MB church. These influential leaders chose the "immersion only" route to local MB church membership, causing needless heartache for many people including myself. Later in my youth, I was baptized via the pouring practice in the GC church. Many years later, moving to another "beautiful" Province, as a family we "shopped churches," deciding on joining an MB church where most members had not heard of "immersion only" regulations. We attend a MB church today!

It could be argued that since the wrongs committed during this period of time in our lives in Spears school district were in the past, and best left unsaid. Yes, the "wrongs committed"

were some fifty years later formally recognized by the MB conference. The MB conference officials asked the "other conferences" for forgiveness for these misdeeds, committed for the
most part by a few, yet influential leaders, mostly having
occurred in southern Manitoba. The "other conferences"
accepted the forgiveness request. Both conferences were joined
on the same platform, seeking God's guidance, in prayer and
embraces of both conference leaders, it was reported. Today, to
my knowledge, the matter is sealed in the past as I understand
it. In my mind that's the case, but nevertheless a factor in my
youth that I am writing about!

It is my understanding that in Manitoba today, where the
majority of these "misguided instances" occurred, the younger
people of the MB church and the General Conferences churches
have "trampled the fences" that this issue created eons ago.
Today it is common that church functions are often mingled
with the conference affiliations not evident. Likely most young
Christians are unaware of the past difference! Praise the Lord!

My attempt is, as it is on all stages of my Mennonite
upbringing, that I document in this book, *Rappelling the
Mennonite Mountain*, a description of the affects, the strains and
strength these "misdeeds" may have or did impact the lives of
many living in the Spears school district area.

In Spears school, kids attended from many different
Mennonite church backgrounds. There was the Rudnerwiede,
Sommerfelder, Bergthaler, Old Colony, and the MB church.
The MB church leaders were by my account, "The tempest in
the tea pot." All the other church members were content to
accept each other's place of worship as an equal, a matter of one's
choosing. The mode of baptism varied in this church mix, some
baptized by pouring the water on the head of the believers, while
others choose to use the sprinkle form of baptism. These "other

churches" respected each other's modes of this sacred event, which the Bible is not clear on as to the mode, leaving that mode open to Christian choice. The Bible is however very clear that baptism is to be a desire of each Christian. Baptism is an outward sign of what has happened inside a person.

These different views of baptism were carried into the Spears school and fermented by an overzealous teacher. The majority of students were from other than MB churches. With an "immersion stance" teacher promoting the immersion method, as the "correct and only mode," the minority became like the majority, a pious one at that in my view! In today's lingo, this teacher's behavior would likely have qualified for a new term, the Christian bully!

How did such a non-related school issue become a school issue? That was the question as a youngster I asked myself, other students, my own parents many times! The answers from the parents were guarded as parents of GC background attempted to have normal, friendly relationships in their living area. It should be said that some MB families did not like the MB stance taken by the local MB church, but remained silent in public, expressing their dislike of the issue in private to us. For many years, while these different views on form of baptism were present in the Spears school district resident's minds, strangely they remained a more subtle issue off the school property. Neighbour helping neighbour, some home to home visiting occurred, despite these veiled differences. Not all MB neighbours shared these strong immersion views and, rather than live with the conflict, pulled up stakes, relocating to another part of the province. While the immersion controversy may not have been the only incentive to relocate, it certainly seemed to be a part of the equation.

Even before I was of school age, my older siblings began coming home with questions and comments that had been made to them in school regarding baptism modes. To my understanding, the extra half-hour that had had foisted on students by the Trustees of the day was to be the study of the German language, certainly not a promo for a certain Church! The line between the two, language study and religion, was paper thin, and thus easily crossed.

Most parents, as did mine, taught peace and tolerance in traditional Mennonite fashion. The Bible was the true Word of God! While at times different interpretations of Scripture promoted discussions, these served as a form of spiritual growth. Discussions took place at family gatherings and neighbour visits. When tolerance is present in each person's mind, others views respected, a healthy form of discourse most often results in rich relationships.

Religion was the cornerstone of being a Mennonite! My grandfather (Mom's Dad) and his parents had moved about from Holland to Russia, finally to Canada, in order to practice the religion of choice openly and freely. Thousands of Mennonites died for their religious beliefs in countries like Russia and Holland, plus other countries, in decades past. These situations of yesteryear had been overheard in discussions, while visiting friends having lived through this turmoil in other countries. My mind kept mulling the question, why should a mode of adult baptism become an issue in a country as fine as Canada? The act of baptism is very clearly endorsed by Scripture, while the mode of baptism allows for discretion.

What brought this dormant view to the front burner of the Flatfields area and more pointedly the Spears school district was the hiring of a certain schoolteacher. Mr. and Mrs. Epp, with their four children, moved into the old teacherage in "Spears school campus." The family was a friendly lot, coming highly recommended from the scant information provided by past teaching post districts. Later, what appeared to have been "a hidden agenda," the baptism mode issue came to light!

School began in September as per normal but it soon became very apparent, even to my young eyes, that "MB kids" would be allowed to dominate. Mr Epp, it turned out, was not only a MB church member, but held a very strong view that only immersion baptism was valid! All other believers that were not immersed in baptism, should all be re-baptized to be eligible to enter heaven, according to Mr. Epp's overzealous mind on this subject. Later in life we of course learned that baptism is not a requirement to enter heaven, but at the time this was taught as a must. The thief on the cross beside Jesus is proof that baptism is not a firm requirement for eternal life. As Jesus upon hearing the thief repent of his sins while dying on the Cross, and recognized Jesus as the Saviour of the world, was told by Jesus "Thou shalt be with me in paradise"!

In fairness, Mr Epp did live an exemplary everyday lifestyle, being well-versed in Scripture teachings. But the fact that he was a promoter, if not a ringleader, of this immersion-only theory cannot be overlooked. Not only did he hold this view on baptism, the Epps were a part of a few families in the local MB Church that seemed to hold the same baptism mode view. Whether Mr. Epp was the "brain child" of this errant theory regarding baptism, or a strong follower of leaders in the local MB church promoting this hypothesis was not clear to me. Attempts to be somewhat subtle about his stance on the baptism promulgate did not make the grade! Mr. Epp found it a challenge not to express his polarized view on the subject in the thirty-minute time allotted each day for German language, in the Speers classroom.

The Government's permission that had been granted to Mennonites, before they immigrated to Canada, that religious freedom and language taught could be exercised in school. The condition however from the Provincial Education department was that the half-hour religion and German language option would need to be conducted in other than the normal 9 a.m. to 4 p.m. school hours.

Mennonites, being early risers (parents at least), decided that an 8:30 a.m. school start would be the choice. Mennonites also believed that hard work was not only good for the young people, it was Scriptural as well! Hard work to Mennonites appeared to be akin to "making love to a widow—it's hard to overdo"! Therefore after four o'clock activities were not to be of a school nature, but rather farm work related!

"Earning your bread by the sweat of your brow" was a motto well practised in our family! Enjoying nature or checking out a new bird's nest on the way home from school required an explanation for the tardiness. Futile, though, it was to explain one's reason for being a few minutes later, since a straight line between school and home was point "A" and "B"! Any other delays were a "C" and a "C" was not permitted in the report card or on the route home from school!

A quick snack was waiting at home or at least we could inspect the offerings Mom's pantry displayed. A Mennonite pantry was a separate walk-in room off the kitchen. Mostly a homemade bun, with cookies being available on occasion but, the prying eyes of a sister would likely result in dropping the second or third cookie I had in my palm! Failing to do so, you ran the risk of being reported to Mom! A double cookie never kept me from enjoying a full supper two hours later! My sister, (a walking thermometer figure) could not comprehend the stocky bod that I displayed! I lived by the adage that "skinny people don't live longer, it only seems longer"! Love you Sis'!

Should my route home from school having been "A" to "B" and a "C," the pantry sojourn was likely cancelled due to lack of time, so I was informed. Sis', who jostled me out the pantry with the standard "I'll tell Mom" threat, she was free to nibble, undetected in the house, while I was compelled to do chores! I digress.

At Spears school, Monday mornings thirty minutes of "Bible lessons or German language" often amounted to a review of the happenings in the MB church the day before! Since only the MB families had been in attendance, it was these kids that were in "Mr. Epp's story circle," while the majority of us were compelled to listen to these "gladiators of the day before"! In fairness, some MB kids disapproved of such tactics, but most had a jolly reunion, while the rest of the students waited impatiently for the real classes to commence!

Had a baptism taken place on Sunday in the MB church, then the Monday thirty minutes special class could turn into forty-five minutes before the gloating and "halo polishing" subsided! It was strange how the invitations to such MB events were freely given to all the kids. On occasion when a fellow student was baptized, we did take in the MB baptism services. However the reverse, when we invited the MB kids to an event in our church, it had "slipped their minds" or their MB church had another "world beater service" they could not miss! Our church world was clearly "off limits" in their thoughts! Second class we were, by a country mile in their minds!

It takes little imagination to see that with a teachers mindset such as Mr. Epp's was in regards to MB activities, the students from the same MB mindset would have the "superior" essay results, enjoy the lead parts in school plays, you run with this one!

Years later another teacher with an "MB bent" gave me this memory. As an example, when on a music test (my weak subject) was given on the black board, I approached the teacher's desk, stating that the music bar and notes given were a contradiction or, bluntly put, an error! No correct answer could be arrived at was my message. The miffed teacher snorted at my audacity to make such a claim, as he considered himself to be "Mr. Music"! As this was the main portion of the test, I handed in my test paper, with the "corrected bar," quite prepared to flunk the subject if I was proven incorrect. The teacher was taken back by my unprecedented actions of handing in my test paper with the "corrected music bar," as I saw it. Mr. Music inquired of the other mostly "MB" students, if they had any difficulty understanding the music score as it was given on the blackboard. Most of the students had answered the question without difficulty, they claimed, leaving me to the scorn of wearing the dunce cap!

The teacher presented me with my unfinished work, giving me a second chance to recant in the face of my defeat at the hands of the music knowledgeable student toadies. I refused, stating I was prepared to stand by my contention that what was asked on the test question on the blackboard was impossible to answer correctly to my limited music knowledge. The invisible dunce cap placed on my head by my peer students, as well as the teacher, may have acted as a "tourniquet" on my better judgement! It is likely that I displayed some defiance as I sat undeterred in my gnarled old desk.

With a flair of satisfaction, displaying his authority, the teacher announced to the class my disqualification from the exam! He asked me to leave the school at once, as I was considered a distraction to the other students. I complied with his request, leaving the building, debating whether to go home or stay for what I felt could become "round two" should the teacher realize his blunder!

Sitting on the school porch steps, pondering my bold actions, and consequences that would surely follow, I mulled the music question over and over in my mind, arriving at the same answer I had given on my test paper each time. My first anger had subsided, in fact, a pensive mood had taken anger's place, as I sat on the splintered wooden porch, not knowing what was running through the teacher's mind.

Recess soon followed, with the uneasy teacher now checking to see if I had gone home. I asked him, on my precious recess time, if I could explain my stance. Knowing the high value I placed on my recess time, the teacher became somewhat unglued by my request, stammering a shaky "why, sure!"

The anger that I thought had left in favour of the more desirable pensive mood, had only been placed in abeyance, the incense was pushing the envelope again!

With chalk in hand, I showed the teacher the flaw in his music stanza, creating a contradiction or an impossibility to answer. Deathly silence set in! I had the teacher on the run! Yes, I had lost my cool! If a correction was to come from the teacher, I wanted him to have to do so in front of the same class he had totally demolished me in only minutes ago! I left to enjoy the remaining minutes of recess, considering that my point had been made, although "enjoy" is overstating the case a bit. My fellow schoolmates, still thinking they held a winning hand in the music test, treated me like I had become a piranha. "He who laughs last, laughs longest," I told myself as I prepared my mind for round two after recess! Class recalled, the teacher announced that the music test had been cancelled, a re-write of the now corrected music bar would allow the other students a second chance. My blood boiled! That pensive mood that had made a brief appearance as I sat on the back porch was now being crowded into the unused portion of the brain, at least when you are tied up losing your cool! I had redrawn my answer (correctly) on my test paper before handing it in, now feeling entitled to have it marked and returned to me as well as the other students test papers, at that moment I hoped with a failing mark for my piranha shy classmates! Secondly, by canceling the exam, I surmised he hoped to save face, not having to render an open verdict on the music exam in front of the entire class!

Also it was a safe assumption that my fellow students, who had claimed to understand the question perfectly, when the teacher sought to embarrass me in front of my peers, had answered incorrectly; there is no right answer to a wrong question!

The teacher knew he had riled me, I was not to be appeased! Perhaps the teacher feared his handling of the matter might be an item for discussion at the next school board meeting. Within minutes, I received my short test paper on my desk with a 92% mark, delivered by a red-faced teacher, red-faced by his anger! A "snot-nosed kid," a non-MB to be sure, had bested him! An apology, too much to ask for? The teacher assumed I would be a happy camper with an unprecedented high mark in music, which I was! He was however badly wrong on the next move. The teacher, now wearing the unemployed dunce cap (in my mind), announced the other students would be allowed a re-write of the examination, with my correct answer still on the blackboard for all to see and copy! My sweaty hand, which was guided by a hot head, shot up like a flare! The just-announced rewrite of the exam, cancelled before my raised hand was acknowledged!

My hand raised again was acknowledged this time, with my request for me leaving school early granted without debate or quiz! The teacher was just too glad to see my ample bod leave the school building!

Although I did not arrive home earlier, but I could now check out that bird's nest in a tree on the route home and still be on time at the pantry door for my cookie allowance, no questions asked. Pup joined me as I strolled across the yard to retrieve the cows for milking. It had been a good day, I deduced, a teacher having accepted submission and secondly I had also proven that my hand was faster than Sister's eye in the pantry. Pup also enjoyed his ration, knowing that my allowance of cookies had not suffered as a result of his enjoying a few of the tasty morsels.

In case I sound as though I was denied food, wrong! My thrill came, when I was being watched for whatever reason or excuse, then beating the system with an additional cookie or three!

My philanthropy, generally reserved for your fellow man, had a broader horizon with me, Pup being my main beneficiary!

Winning was a sweet victory for me but also realizing that it's one thing to win the battle but losing the war is likely when you were from the wrong side of the "church tracks"! Many things I have been accused of in school, however, teacher's pet, never!

Instances of "teacher's pet," as the above case indicates, occurred, resulting in the trustees rotating the teacher from MB to "other" and "other" to MB again! Three trustees were on the school board and they too were rotated with the MB having two one term and "others" one. The reverse occurred at the next election with no open fanfare or animosity. Which does prove my point that there was a strong "undercurrent" even in the adults, MB versus others! It was however a tad more subtle than the MB teacher was in class!

Mennonites can be an interesting bunch! I might add that despite the teacher rotation from MB to other, I still did not ever achieve the status of "teachers pet"! This puzzlement I leave for my readers to decide, why my mantle piece is devoid of such an Oscar!

In fact, it was remarkable that although baptism was a large factor in school, the parents were not openly affected. Friendly relationships remaining intact in the neighbourhood was a huge credit to all concerned. Flatfields was a good area for a Mennonite boy to grow up in, despite the "baptism" situation described. While I, along with many others, would that it had not occurred, history is there, no doubt it will vary in people's memories. Omitting such a saga from this literary recollection would have discomforted me, just as including it did cause me to wince a tad, to spell it out in print. It's behind us, I harbour no ill will; it is however history as I recall it.

School was not all work and study, or debate religion. The Department of Education sponsored a round of films to be shown in schools. Movies were not a part of our Mennonite upbringing. I, for one, did not see a movie in a theater till after I was a married man. I however had gone to the Annual John Deere shows sponsored by the local dealer. These comedy films amused me greatly. So it was with great delight that a stranger knocked on our school door in the dead of winter and said he was here to show us the movies or films. The stranger was a Mr. McLeod. He had parked his car on the main road, having walked the quarter mile to school since the snow banks blocked the short road to school. We had no hydro, therefore his car contained a gas driven power generator to fire up the movie projector. The challenge was to get the car to the school over the snow banks, so the cables from the gas generator would connect with the projector inside. Mr. McLeod was a gutsy man (unlike our teacher), was determined to show the films to us. He chose to break a trail across our frozen farm field and sneak up to the school that way. Alas the power cables were too short from where the car was parked.

Mr. McLeod checked the hardened snow banks and asked the school lads to push. The male students almost carried the Model A Ford across the snow banks some ten feet high, our gutless teacher shaking his head. Screen set up, generator running, the show was on, with the car being on "a high" in this instance—snow bank that is. For many, these were the first movies they had ever seen. I believe it was Abbott and Castello, Woody Woodpecker, plus some educational films, which I fortunately forgot long ago. It was a fine afternoon for all the students. When the films were done, we again carried Mr. McLeod's car back to the road and regretfully, never did see him again.

Author's note:

The feelings expressed regarding the MB stance on baptism was the view of a young man in the six- to twelve-year-old range.

In "fast forward" let me say that, reading Mennonite church history years later, the Mennonite Church waded through more turmoil on many issues than one can imagine! Likely more turmoil from 1920 through 1940 than in any other time on Canadian soil than it has prior or anytime thereafter. The mode of baptism was but one of the myriad of controversies and challenges the churches faced.

Only God's hand of blessing upon the leaders of these factions could have brought the conclusions we enjoy today!

Fairfield class of '47

More Education in Overalls

*A*t about eight years of struggling on this planet, you begin to accept the fact that life is all about tradeoffs. School to begin and a new teacher to put through the paces, but the summer was now pretty much a write-off.

School meant I might have less farm chores to do, or at least attempt to get out of doing them. But the trade off was sitting in school and studying at least some boring subjects! But then there was recess, the buddies and the stories to catch up on. Many of the students wore hand-me downs and I was one that had some of that in my life. I was fortunate in that I was short and stubby, while my older Bro was skinny and tall, so for the most part it was a no-go for his cast-off clothes, because of fit. Calvin Klein or Bugle jeans were not invented yet, but my folks did want to send a decently dressed kid to school. New clothes were always nice, but that trade off! Going shopping for these new duds and the "correct fit" of the inside leg!

"Duds" consisted of new bib overalls, a shirt or two (if they were on sale at Gladstones), a new pair of shoes. The shoes, of course, would be for Sunday best wear only, the now Sunday shoes were relegated into the daily ones that I wore to school. All this may sound fine on the surface, but the fitting of these new overalls! That was the trade off and humiliating part of the process.

The fitting room at Gladstones, for young lads like me, was behind some large boxes. Being an all-male staff at Gladstones, I could not deliver a valid argument, it seemed, to not change clothes in a semi-private area of cardboard boxes. The new overalls were slipped on and the pant legs were always too long, a given with me, but Mom would hem those suckers *likity-split*! The "fit" of the overalls was the part I just detested! Those dreaded words "How is the crotch area?" was Mom's favorite line. The answer I gave had not an iota of bearing on the result! Mom had to check for herself! I cannot recall an overall being rejected ever because of "the crotch" being this or that, why the aggravation? Secondly, if I had said, "much too tight" it would have meant the next size larger, the pant legs longer, the pant pockets lower after hemming! There were no slims or barrel-chest sizes, it was small, medium and large, the crotch area be damned! Thirdly, if I may, there is no Low German word for *crotch* that I know of, or used in our household. So Mom's question meant "the crotch area" but her words, translated into English, were "how are they between the legs?" Assuming that "they" meant the trousers, yes Mom, "they" are fine! Mom reached for my "inside leg" to check something that could not be changed or corrected, I objected! Knowing full well if the fit should prove a challenge later, Mom would recite line and verse to me of my silly refusal to not allow her to pinch and pull! I resolved that issue by my refusal, never again did I have to re-visit that situation with Mom! All future trouser fittings I was in total command of "they," in fact we now used the adult term of "fit"!

The shoes, well, they were kinda fun. Gladstones, being on the cutting edge of 1940's technology, had brought in a foot X-ray machine. It worked neat while it lasted. You stuck your foot in the bottom opening on the platform, with your shoe on. You could see your foot, bones, and even wiggle your toes, seeing it through a sort of viewfinder at the top. Mom and Dad had a good look; if the machine had not broke down yet, it was my turn to peek.

The machine was however soon to bite the dust, as it were. The government decided that the X-ray was leeching dangerous rays that could cause foot cancer. So much better that you cramp your feet into a poorly selected shoe than a "maybe"-cancer-causing proper fit. Likely was a good move by the government but I hated to see the machine go. To date I am not aware of any "foot cancer" in the Winkler area because of the X-ray machine. None of the other kids at school had heard of this fantastic new X-ray gadget. It was fun to be on the cutting edge of this Mennonite world! Yes, you could cut the tension with a baseball bat!

Manure? It's actually used oats-hay-straw combo—used for cook stove.

The Merry Jolly Season

*C*hristmas was my favorite time of year, rating just about even with threshing season!

It was the season when one was reminded what the true meaning of Christmas was, the birth of Jesus Christ.

However, my folks were not prudes about Christmas. Yes, "Jesus was the reason for the Season," but on the fun side of Christmas there was room for the mythical Santa Claus. The first few years of my life, they played the Santa Claus stuff on me. Although it sounded hokey to me right out of the gate, I enjoyed the idea that Santa had come down the chimney. Nah, it did not make sense because Dad had said at other times of the year that our chimney was in poor shape and had some loose brick obstructions, etc.

Either the third or fourth Christmas of my life, their cover was blown; I knew it was the parents as the gift-givers, after all, the spare upstairs room had been off limits to me since early November. For me, handling both concepts was not a problem and we had good laughs over the mythical Santa.

Falling asleep on the eve of the twenty-fourth was a challenge for me for many a Christmas Eve.

All our gifts were given on the twenty-fifth, early morning. There were times when on the twenty-fourth in the evening, I felt I did not fall asleep at all so great was the anticipation. Mom and Dad, thinking or hoping we kids had fallen asleep, could be heard making many trips down the stairs as they hauled the "loot" from the spare room down to the kitchen table. Here the stacks of toys were placed, approximately where we would sit for our meals, each of the kids at a separate location.

A definite time that we kids could come downstairs on the twenty-fifth, was not given, but before 4 a.m. would not have been kind, according to the older, problem siblings. As for me, I would have liked to help the folks carry the haul downstairs, *"for-botan"!* By about 4 a.m. or so, I either got roused or I roused the others, and we kids could, at long night's last, head downstairs to our waiting bounty! Well, almost! It was still oil lamps at our house, the older Brother and Sister combo had to go downstairs first, under the guise of having to light the lamp, before I was allowed come down. This again was a first class farce against chubby! It seemed to take forever before they returned. I suspected (correctly) that the lamp was well lit, Sis and Bro were checking out the goodies, making me wait just to remind me that I was number four in the line up! I put up with some delay but then I simply bounded down the stairs with all the usual threats of them telling the folks and all the toys would be sent back that I had gotten. I knew full well that it poppycock and bravado! I was too busy digging into my booty to give them the time of day! Our gifts were not wrapped (waste of money to Mennonites) thus we could eyeball the loot in one swoop. Our folks were very generous and all us kids received plenty of gifts.

Always, a large bowl had been set at each kids spot; this bowl was filled with peanuts, candies and nuts. All mixed together, made for some peanut shells on some candies but that's how the little paper bags came at school as well. In fact, I still had some brown peanut shells lodged on my back molars from sucking on a candy from the school treats. Mandarin oranges were plenty at our house and they came in the wooden box, which was set in the middle of the large table for all to partake of.

The wooden tinker toy set, the farm tractor and implements, all items that I had on my wish list! An entire set of heavy metal farm animals from Eaton's, many of these toys I have some sixty years later, even the wind up toys do work. Our kids and grandkids, just waiting for me to croak, have tagged all these items. You did hear the story of the grandson that requested his Papa to croak like a frog. Papa went along with puzzling request and croaked for that favorite grandson. Finally, Papa felt an explanation about this strange "croak" request was over due. "Why do you ask me to croak?" Papa requested. The grandson says, "Well granny says we will all go to Hawaii after you croak!" All too soon it was 8 a.m., and the cows, horses, and chickens required feeding. The chickens lay eggs even on Christmas Day that has to be gathered.

Most times we were not asked to go to church on December twenty-fifth, as we had for all of December heard the Christmas message. This gave us some more playtimes with the toys. Sleeping in for the folks was not possible, as our noises that had been contained or muffled grew louder, and my tractor, when fired up, was quite disruptive; it was Christmas! I insisted in my early years to go show the folks what "Santa" had brought. They blew the Santa theory by a tad sleepy and irritant voice, saying they had seen the whole works.

Some years, the family gathering on Mom's side of the family was the twenty-fifth. Other years the twenty-six. How this rotation was arrived at, I never did catch on to. Dad's side of the family took the safe route, with the gathering on what Mennonites called "the third holiday" or the twenty-seventh of December. If it was the twenty-fifth for Mom's side, that posed a problem for me. I had just done my chores, was totally engrossed in my toys when the announcement was made to clean up get dressed, off to Granny's house we went! With ample fuss, but then parents are not a democracy, it's a dictatorship, you know who won the day!

Into the sedan car we piled, with lots of animal fur blankets to keep us warm. Heaters in cars were there, but mostly in name only. On real thirty-below winter days, Dad would have placed baseball sized rocks in the kitchen bake oven the night before. These warm-to-hot stones were now placed inside the animal blankets at our tootsies. This helped greatly to keep our digits warm, and then seven people in a four-seated car made for a "warm," compact relationship. We were some of the first to arrive at Grandma and Grandpa's house. Also the first ones to leave for home and the farm chores, later in the day.

Grandparents did have a large house but even that filled up quickly! Sixteen kids my Grandparents had, with fifteen coming home for Christmas, the one lived in far away BC. I never did count the "herd" of cousins!

The main meal, yes, they all came hungry; it was high noon. It was basic Mennonite-style eating; the men come first. This demanded a table setting or two of the adult male species, then the famished kids and some mommies did sneak in a bit. The table held fifteen to twenty persons at one time, depending on the squeeze chosen, combined with the whining one did! The meal was basic Mennonite type, with *"Pluma-moos"* (Plum soup) and roast pork. Turkey was not raised on their farm and you served whatever animal meat you raised. If Grandma saw the soup pots wearing down on the hot stove, a few large ladles of water were added without any fanfare, known as a "soup stretcher."

While the men were eating, the women were urging them on, to cut the visiting and move to the large living room for the gabfests, of which there were many. Must say that some of my uncles were rather "boorish" about slow eating and visiting. Oh yes, they made sure they were at the first table for the food, but then turned very inconsiderate for the kids and women waiting behind them to also dine! I was always proud of my dad when he was at the table, eating first. He would eat and urge others to do so, and then he would be first to ask the others to move so he could get out from behind the long table and chair setup. Some uncles grumbled, but Dad was persistent and managed to get the "boors" to move to the living room!

One set of "moms" was now washing the dishes from the men's setting, new settings were placed for the next crew to dine. To call this houseful a zoo was an understatement! The well-fed men in the living room had bowls of peanuts and candies to tide them over till *faspa* (lighter Mennonite lunch) would happen. The peanut shells were all deposited on the lino floor for sweeping later. Eating was a non-stop event at such gatherings!

Finally at about 2:30 p.m. the main meal completed as were the dishes. It was that dreaded time when the grandkids were expected to recite from memory a poem learned in school for the annual Christmas school program, but now the critics listening were the uncles, aunts and other snickering cousins.

Grandma and Grandpa did what was expected of them, sitting side by side on a couch as the grandkids recited their offerings. Some cousins, in lieu of reciting a poem, stood in front of the grandparents and bawled till they felt they had paid their dues and walked away to receive their Christmas bag. Then they resumed their bully tactics in the other room with the cousins, it was a scam!

Speaking of scams, was the tradition of giving the grandkids some cash. Grandma and her two youngest daughters had managed to pick some favourites from the flock of grandkids.

A Mennonite specialty was to call your only son, *"Sonn."* This moniker then stuck with the kid and with other cousins, at times other cousins not even knowing the kid's real name. The silly correction or the revealing of the kid's real name came, when he was to be married. Can you imagine the Minister saying, "Do you take this 'Sonn' as your wedded Husband?" That aside, my frustration came in that there were two "Sonns" in two different families, both being Grandma's fair-haired boys. So when the coins were passed out, "Sonn and Sonn" were each given a quarter, while others cousins were compelled to appreciate a thin dime! We were shushed up when attempting to seek an ombudsman to even the playing field. "It goes by age," we were sent packing with, but our birth certificate did not bear this out! The value between a quarter and a dime was huge, when you are ten years old, and a buck was still a buck! This recital program involved a half-hour or more.

Some of the first dinner table men were now making loud comments that it was coffee time. The dutiful women took the bait and the first table of men was again topping up their tummies with gallons of coffee, breads and jams. The coffee had to be with lots of rich farm cream and sugar cubes by the handful! Cookies came in handfuls of six or so. On the second pass, a modest three was taken, to display restraint!

When the burping got a bit much, the ladies again had to urge those lazy uncles into the living room, allowing others to have a bite before it was time to say goodbye. Each grandchild received a small bag of candies, peanuts and an orange! Different house, same drill as at home!

Grandparents' bedroom that had served as the "grandkids' room" for the afternoon resembled a war torn area of this globe! Being a large bedroom with two double beds that had served as a trampoline for all was showing the nature of the activity.

Someone got hurt, another lost his Christmas goodie bag, and the tears flowed. Another kid had snaffled a loose bag and was busy filling his face with the newly scammed loot. Outerwear clothing had been on the one bed, was now strewn over the floor; the missing mitten department was on overload! I was glad when Dad beckoned me to get my jacket on; take me home where some sanity was possible!

Goodbyes were thrown about as we made our way to the frozen car. The car required a push by human manpower down the hill from the large yard, and the motor sprang to life as Dad manipulated the standard gearshift.

An hour later we were home and ran through the chore list as fast as possible. Some playtime again, but the sandman arrived early and I succumbed to his wishes!

A bright sunshine greeted us next morning, after my mammoth sleep. Sunshine on a prairie winter day should not be construed as nice weather, this day proved that point. It was somewhere in the thirty-below temperature range. Dad came inside the house for a kettle of hot water, as the artesian well in the barn that supplied all the cattle with salty water had frozen and would not flow. One boiling kettle of water, the tap spewed forth its salty liquid. On such cold days the cattle were not too keen on drinking much cold water, but rather indulged on the feed given them. Milk supply also reflected the weather and production was down.

Straw had been hauled into the barn and stacked before Christmas, which made chore time a quickie. As I climbed the frosty vertical ladder to the barn hayloft, our neighbour's cat hissed as he beat a hasty retreat from his perch on our female cat. Despite the frosty day, romance was in full bloom! I pitchforked the hay down the opening in the floor into the hay shed in the barn.

Soon we were again inside the warm house, an entire day to play as I pleased, which I did.

Meals at Christmas time on a non-event day, as this December twenty-sixth, Mom declared a help yourself deal, which I liked. With all the candy and peanuts one could be called to account at a full table when you burp before the meal. This non-accountability suited me just fine.

By afternoon, the novelty of all the new toys dimmed somewhat, and Pup was beckoning through the window with his hopeful fluffy tail wagging. I bundled up real warm with scarf and huge mitts; making Pup's Christmas as I emerged from the warm house. I put the small harness on Pup and hitched him to my sled. Not what he really had in mind, it appeared, but he towed me across the yard several times before we decided to just check out the hen-laying barn. The fish Dad was baking in the summer kitchen stove was ready and I served the hens that special treat they had missed for the past few days. Chores done, it was time to play the Monopoly game I had received as a gift from the folks.

Next day, December twenty-seventh, was what Mennonites called "the third holiday;" it was time to visit Grandma on Dad's side of the family, the "Town Grandma" we called her.

The commercial stores were open for the most part but to us it was a "religious holiday," that in fact has no Biblical basis that I became aware of, on second thought does some of the other holidays? It served as an excellent time for the Mennonites to catch up on some visitations that were long overdue. Mennonites were hard workers, but when the time was right they knew how to use a few laid-back days.

Mennonite "extra" holidays included "The three wise men arriving at the Crib of Jesus," which shut the commercial stores down January sixth. The other holiday is in spring, depending on the date of Easter, and forty days hence from Easter was Jesus' ascension into Heaven. On these days the Mennonite towns were shut tight. Max Gladstone, our favourite Jewish merchant, used the day as a purchasing day in the city, which was open. Max used to poke a bit at our Mennonite holidays. He would say, "Every time three guys get on a camel at the same time, you Mennonites shut down the stores." As a Jew, the Gladstone family also celebrated the Jewish Holidays, but they did not shut their stores but were absent without any fanfare.

At Town Grandma's house, the atmosphere was quite different than on Mom's side. It was a much smaller, more intimate type of visit. The entire gathering could fit around one table, sharing the food and laughter without a group pushing you to "eat up, move on!" Yes there was a "Rocky Mountain" flavour in the mix, as Dad's brothers also lived in that neck of the woods.

What brought it on is not known, but an orange eating challenge contest broke out amongst the Uncles. A quick trip to downtown, only a few blocks away, large bags of oranges landed on Grandma's table. Grandma could not see the point, but she knew when to back off, let the men make fools of themselves she did, and the men did also! As I got the loosely knit rules, it was not how fast but rather how many oranges they could consume. Dad came in second, with my bloated uncle taking first place.

Liquor was not a factor in any of my relative's homes, which I am aware of but in the afternoon, a bottle of *"snaptes"* did make its rounds for a quick swig. At my tender age, my uncle poured a bit into the bottle cap, looking at my dad, who nodded, I had my first taste of liquor. As I recall it was strong, made my eyes water but requested a second taster. That done pretty much completed my drinking days.

Dad had brought his all-too-little-used violin along this year. Some of my unc's had done the same. Another had a harmonica and a guitar was included in the impromptu band. Dad's violin was a rather unique one, in that it was about thirty percent smaller than a standard violin. The uncles treated us to such lovely Christmas music. Dad's violin proved to be a bit of a sought after instrument, with the entire violin players asking to trade violins with Dad for a number of songs. The jamming went on for hours!

After the Christmas songs were exhausted, they swung into some toe-tapping barn dance numbers. Everyone seemed to lose track of time. When Grandma looked at the kitchen clock, she realized that she would be late with *faspa*. Such a good time was had by musicians as well as audience, that no one seemed to mind waiting for the coffee to perk.

The *faspa* lunch was the traditional bread, jam, cheese and homemade beef sausage, along with the gallons of coffee that was such a must for the adults. While I liked coffee, mostly because it was forbidden at my tender age, my treat was to have coffee poured into the saucer and I then drowned umpteen sugar cubes in the shallow dish. The trick was to watch the coffee soak up the side of the pure white sugar cube and then pop it into your mouth before it disintegrated into the coffee. After you had your sugar quota, a quick glance about and then slurp the remaining sugar laden coffee from the saucer!

Another Mennonite custom I grew up with was that the hot caffeine was poured into your saucer first, allowed to cool a tad and then drank from the saucer. Can you say "slurp"? The goodbye hugs and well-wishes complete, we piled into the frozen car and roared towards Flatfields and that wonderful place that everyone has, home!

Straw Hat Holdups

eing chubby and short is rarely part of a kid's wish list, but when that's the configuration dealt you, can't change it, then work it! I guess that was my approach to my young life. However, I was blessed with a fast body. Often short and chubby is matched with slow and clumsy, not this dude! Winning school races, even in older classes, was a regular occurrence.

My chubby body was also given a chubby or pumpkin-type head. On top of this round noggin I perched a size seven, peaked Mexican straw hat that became part of me. Sure I got sassed and giggled at, but it kept me cool—it did more than that, it got me cold cash! Cash even at a young age had value to me! Soda pop was a nickel, order of fries in a sit-down restaurant (there were no drive-throughs) was ten cents.

Parents allowance was not dependable, at times, yes, other times, no, without an explanation given. A jingle in your jeans on Saturday night drew attention from your peers. Most young lads my age did not know how to make a money decision. They either rarely got to handle money or, if they did, they blew it all at the first opportunity. This chubby owl always had cash in his pockets, due in part to my wise parent owl guidance. It was "real grown-up" to not buy a pop or cone of ice cream when you had the cash in your jeans to make the transaction! Guys would gasp when I said no to something, at times even when they had scooped a nickel from their folks and were parting with it again at first opportunity.

So without a regular allowance, how did I manage to jingle coins? My straw hat and chubby body! Whenever I smelled money, I was willing to hustle!

A wealthy land baron lived several miles away from our homestead, but owned land next to our farm. Roads to his property were really cow trails. After a heavy rain downpour, the trails with its huge, deep mud puddles were for tractors only. Mr. Land Baron wanted to check on his crop on a regular basis, to give his men direction on work required and just keep an eye on his many assets.

Our farm had a good driveway and pasture at the back of the yard. We also had a gate out of our pasture at the far side, next to Mr. Baron's large fields. So Mr. Land Baron came down our dry driveway, requested permission to cut through our pasture onto his massive land tract out the back gate of our pasture. Permission was granted and taken for granted thereafter. Besides the large straw hat, I also had an infectious smile I was told; that Chamber of Commerce, ear to ear grin. Draw your own mental picture: short, stout lad, oversized straw-hat, grin just ready to drip, collie at his side; that's a cash picture!

Once Dad gave Mr. Baron the crossing rights, I was off to the pasture gate as fast as my speedy legs could offer. I opened the gate, allowing the wealthy boy to pass through in his polished new car. Grin in place as he passed by me. The car stopped, as the driver's window rolled down. I was at the window like a magnet draws metal (or coins in this case), my hand in the pocket was already cupped to receive a coin or two. A dime was pressed into my sweaty palm. The grateful straw hat bent forward as he pressed my flesh. The back gate he would need to exit from was 200 yards away but I could handle the exercise, without a word, dashed off to the far gate. Mr. Baron, in his shined car, drove slowly, making sure to miss the fresh cow pats in the pasture as he moved towards the rear pasture gate. I had the barb wire gate open when he arrived, waving him through with a big smile. I knew Mr. Baron would not be very long, and I had open time on my agenda for the day; Pup stayed with me as we sat down, leaning on the gnarled fence post for a breather. My hand in the pocket squeezed the dime to be sure it was real.

Our water dugout was near by, so Pup and myself sauntered over to check on the croaking frogs. About a half-hour later I saw the glossy black car approaching our back gate. Again the gate was open for "Mr. Coin" to pass through. The race to the farmyard gate began immediately, with Pup winning by a nose!

Collies do have long noses, giving Pup the edge on me. The straw hat also demanded some wind resistance, slowing me up a step or two. The open gate allowed the car to go unimpeded onto our yard. The window again rolled down, the straw-hatted looked up into the open car window. Mr. Baron talked me into accepting twenty-five cents this time, a stuttering man would have had equal success! I guess he took time and effort into account as he added up the damage done to my timeline, rewarding me accordingly.

Well, he did not actually talk to me as he handed the quarter to my outstretched hand, but I thought he might. Dad was now back on the scene, chatting with Moneybags! Compliments on my services were expressed to Dad but I had no words to offer. This was the time to remain humble and quiet! As the car gently pulled away I gave my "banker" the two-fingered salute, as in come again, or "V" for victory salute! Churchill was still a hero at this time!

I was the talk of the farm, thirty-five cents was more than an hour's wage for a grown man at that time!

Alas, I had overplayed my hand a bit. Big brother had his nose out of joint over the cash I had received.

Big boy suggested a sharing arrangement. "No way," was my answer; it was my grin, my straw hat, and my legs, err brains, that caused all this good fortune to be bestowed on me. The subject died, kinda.

A few weeks later the situation repeated itself, Mr. Baron pulled up in that chrome-lined black car of his, but the difference this time was that he had Mrs. Baron with him. "Show time," I said to myself! The gate opened, the straw hat tipped forward as they passed through to their acreage, my grin was lit like sunshine! The window rolled down, Mr. Baron knew that this was a good time to be a bit more generous. After all, he was a man of stature in the area, Mrs. Baron should not have to chide him or remind him of that fact! Also, the tolls are always higher when you have an extra passenger with you, I thought; as the window opened he pressed that quarter into my hand. The programmed straw hat repeated its established routine. I was waiting at the far gate as the car purred through. The dug out, Pup, frogs; same thing, different day! An open gate greeted the Barons as they passed through. Pup again beat me to the next gate, to allow the undisturbed passage for the royal couple's exit. I was holding Pup by the mane as another quarter hit my hand. Again, my trademarked two-fingered salute and an extra flutter of my stubby fingers to Mrs. Baron as they rode off. I released my hold on Pup as he gently lowered his raised hind leg. Pup accepted the defeat without acrimony. All of Pup's taste was in his mouth, as he showed no respect for chrome spoke wheels versus the regular wooden jobs on most cars. Pup was uncouth in the chivalry department.

Lunchtime soon followed, but the news of my money-laundering scheme had preceded me as I approached the lunch table. Fifty cents for less than an hour of my time, this called for a family summit meeting! Mom's "fair haired boy," also known as my older brother, was miffed! Wealth sharing was on his agenda! Rather than share the quick cash, but knowing I had to compromise, I suggested we take turns when Mr. Baron arrives again. I felt pretty safe in my assumption that without my chubby body, hat and hustle, the window on the car might not roll down at all. The bait was accepted, Big Bro had the next turn, which arrived only a week hence. I was out of sight, peeking through the cracks in the barn door. Big Bro opened the gate, the window remained up, but Mr. Baron took a page from my playbook, giving Big Bro a broad smile and wave! The return trip netted the same negative result. Steamed, miffed, and defeated was Big Bro! I emerged from the barn after wiping that smirk off my face long enough to remind Big Bro from a distance that I had the next go, whenever that would be. Big Bro's "crop failure" received little note at the lunch table.

The crop was ripening when Mr. Baron again showed up. I was in place with Pup on my five-fingered leash, meaning a tight hand on his mane. The gate opened, the car stopped, the window rolled down, the hat tipped forward quickly, so as to reveal my smile. The dime in my pocket felt cool in more ways than one! The return trip yielded a quarter, which was added to my growing piggy bank. The message was clearly received by Big Bro. No hat, no grin, dog on the loose adds up to no quarters or dimes! I now had an exclusive on the tollgate!

My piggy bank had other sources of revenue. On a recent visit to Dad's Uncle, the kindly "old man" took me on his knee. He expressed his appreciation for "short little boys" (today an expression like that might cause concern, not way back when),

a quarter also found its way into my hand. I had learned a lesson
from Mr. Baron's money, keep your mouth shut! Other relative
visits produced more "chubby compliments" and requests for a
look at my straw hat, which normally had Sunday off. This
showing of the hat turned into a cash cow for me. For the most
part the donations received were kept low-key but my plump
piggy bank did raise suspicions. Uncle visits were quite frequent
and so were the quarters.

Another unexpected revenue stream came by complete surprise! Visiting my "Town Granny" was always a treat for me.
Living in town, you just had it made! Hydro, telephone, no
chores to do, this had to be easy street! Much as the visits were
fun, they could also be somewhat boring. No dog, no room to
run or bat a ball. Also no roaming about, chasing a few gophers.

I requested from my folks that I be allowed to explore the
sidewalks on the rather short street. Sidewalks were wooden slats
at that time, with a fair amount of ups and downs due to the ter-
rain, warping and dis-repair. This could result in splinters on the
knees and hands if a young lad was, as he ought to be, running!
Granny overhearing the permission granted me, after the regular
warnings about being careful, etc., she now revealed another concern. Two houses down was a tiny white house with a large yard.
Everything was immaculate, as in manicured! House was in perfect paint repair, with the front gate to be respected. This caught
my attention, listening carefully, as Granny, while speaking well
of Mr. Enns who lived there, could not overstate the fact that he
was not to be trifled with, especially kids! His next-door neighbours were a rangy-tang bunch, including the parents and seven
kids. Their yard, a sharp contrast to Mr. Enns finely kept one. In
the neighbour's yard were old car bodies, chicken crates, weeds
galore. Mr. Enns was therefore labeled as a "kid-hater" and did
have a running battle with the untidy neighbours.

Mr. Enns, I learned, was a lifelong, confirmed bachelor, who simply had never met a woman that could match his obsession with neatness and cleanliness. I was on red alert! This could be a way of killing a boring Sunday afternoon. "This guy may not like kids, but that was before he has met me," I said bravely to myself!

Dressed in my Sunday best, I stepped carefully on the uneven wooden sidewalk. Scuffing my Sunday best shoes would not be well received by Mom, since I knew I would be inspected after my sojourn into the unknown. All the warnings were swirling through my hatless, little brain in my rotund head.

Walking past the little white house was precisely as Granny had said, immaculate to a tee! The front gate was closed tight, I could tell without daring to touch it. No decent dog or cat would even consider a shortcut through that yard, I thought. I sauntered back and forth on the sidewalk, which had come as part of the warning package from Granny that those clump footsteps could be annoying to Mr. Enns. I had now reached the end of the street and must return past Mr. Enns' gate and house. Great gads! Mr. Enns was walking from his house to the front gate! A fairly tall, stout man he was, dressed in fine, tidy clothes. His shoes were a sort of slipper type, he must have been relaxing and I may have woke him, I pondered! Running after me was not on his mind with slippers on, I sighed softly. Without my hat I felt disadvantaged to a degree, but shucks, I have my smile! Some of the bravado I had consoled myself with a half-hour ago seemed to have faded several shades. I was going to meet Mr. Enns, ready or not, as he stood by his gate.

My smile broke out with some effort as I approached him. To my surprise, Mr. Enns smiled back. Sure, I thought, this guy is using my tactics! After all, the art of PR is saying "nice doggie, nice doggie," until you have a chance to pick up a rock! Mr. Enns broke the stalemate, "Can you talk Low German?" he

157

asked in his broken English. I answered his question affirmatively in Low German. A broader smile crossed his mustached face. In German he inquired where I was visiting, seemed impressed that I was at my Granny's place two doors down. Where I lived, how often I visited Granny were the next queries. I commented on the nice garden he had. Would I like to walk through the garden with him? When I stammered a bit, he quickly suggested I check with my parents first. "I will be back," I offered in a nervous voice. This guy's fine, I thought.

Half running, but minding the lumpy sidewalk, I made my request known in Granny's house. Some eyes rolled, Granny was shocked! I was given a half-hour window of time to be back.

Skipping, trotting and bouncing my chunky bod back to the waiting Mr. Enns. "Can you tell me when a half-hour is up?" I asked. I was at home in the Low German language as he was. "Sure" was his reply, perhaps more time than he had hoped for; I thought His garden was something to behold! Rows and rows of growing veggies. Not a weed in sight! I declined an offer to pull a carrot, citing my Sunday clothes might attract some dirt. Mr. Enns liked that, a fussy, careful kid, I saw his wheels turning. "Can you come inside?" Now that had not been mentioned at the visiting request from my folks, but what the heck! I was old enough to be a judge of good character and safety! Seven years on this planet had to count for something! "Yes," I said and up the painted wooden steps we went. I offered to remove my shoes, but Mr. Enns said "Just bounce the dust on the porch rug, keep your shoes on."

The house, like his yard and garden, was just so! I was sure a fly would require a visa to get in!

The tiny house had a tiny kitchen and a small living room that had a sofa and chair, plus an end table that held his Holy Bible on a white doily. Mr. Enns sat in his favorite chair and asked me to be comfy on the sofa. My short legs stuck forward as I sat back on the sofa, attempting to appear proper. Farmyard questions dominated the next ten minutes, with Mr. Enns showing interest in my answers by asking more related questions. Mr. Enns saw me glancing at the big ticking clock on the wall. He knew I was a lad of my word and a half-hour was meaningful to me. He reached into the end table drawer, pulling out a chocolate bar. My eyes bulged as I accepted his verbal offer to have it. Mr. Enns expressed pleasure in my visit, suggesting that I come back on the next Granny visit to see him again. As I assured him that I would like to, he pressed a quarter into my hand!

Skippity-hop and I was relaying my good fortune to all at Granny's place. A shocked parentage listened as I unveiled the tale of my good fortune. Granny felt either I was someone very special or a lightning bolt had dumbfounded Mr. Enns! I assured her that I was pretty special with a laugh! My confidence was on high!

Future Granny visits always included a Mr. Enns visit as well. He seemed happy with a short half-hour exchange of thoughts, always having that candy bar and quarter for me. I felt we grew fond of each other, even if the treats had not been there for me. Mr. Enns was a reader and my mom helped me select short story books for him as a Christmas gift. He accepted them, but always reluctantly, expressing the fact that he would rather I just come to see him without gifts. He claimed my repeated visits were a thank you enough.

On occasion we went to visit Granny on a Mennonite type religious holiday, such as Easter Monday or Tuesday. Tuesday, the merchants would be open for business and several times he asked me accompany him for groceries downtown. My folks, for these walking excursions, gave special permission.

I had a silly habit, harmless but noticeable, when I was walking with a grown-up person. Being grown-up was an obsession with me, therefore I did everything grown-ups do, if possible. When walking I would be in lockstep with Mr. Enns; despite his longer legs, I would attempt to take the huge strides he was taking.

Mr. Enns noticed this and commented that "we would make a good marching army with our walking." Not being able to break the habit, Mr. Enns took smaller steps to make me feel an equal.

Our relationship carried on for many years and frankly do not recall when or how the visits ended.

Many years later, after Susan and myself were married, an announcement in the Sunday morning church bulletin requested that a car was needed to take elderly persons to and from church service each Sunday.

We volunteered our services, to our surprise, Mr. Enns was one of the persons seeking this assistance to church and back home. We were glad to help, and for 13 years we drove a car full of elderly people to and from church, which included Mr. Enns.

True to form, Mr. Enns expressed to me that he would only sit beside me in the passenger seat, never to be squeezed into the back seat with perhaps a lady! On one occasion I was under the weather a tad, but we did not want our regular Sunday passengers to miss church. Susan offered to take them to church and home. This she did without a problem, but she did mention that Mr. Enns has seemed somewhat uneasy in the front seat beside her. Next Sunday, Mr. Enns drew me aside in a fatherly fashion and said in future, when ever I was not able to attend church, to just call him and he would stay home. I know some guys are nervous around women but Mr. Enns was several shades on the overcautious side! I naturally accepted this condition requested and remained pleasant friends with him. Susan, who knew Mr. Enns held rigid views, was not offended by his request, to not have her drive him to church! I took her out for dinner!

I assured him that his wish would be honoured, and it was. After so many years of free service to these elderly folks suspicion grew as to whether I was getting some money slipped to me for this service. What did upset me some was when it was suggested that I was "gunning" for Mr. Enns' inheritance, since he had no living relatives. Mennonite rumour mill is always ready to spew out truth or not!

In due course, Mr. Enns did go to his Heavenly reward and I can freely state that I never was offered a dime from Mr. Enns or anyone else while enjoying the rides, nor do I know where his inheritance went. Susan and myself offered a free service to the Lord; it was respected and appreciated. Mr. Enns, on these rides to and from Church, did allude to those special days when I had come over as a youngster, how it had just made his week. During the visits Mr. Enns did tell me of another young lad who also was on his visitation list. Many years later I was to meet this young man in another province and we exchanged similar pleasant memories of Mr. Enns' visits.

To God be the praise and glory!

Blue Sky, Pop and a Sandwich

A blue sky, a nice sheltered hollow—preferably near some bushes—these thoughts will make a young lad take a few risks from the parental department!

Then again, a Sunday afternoon, my collie sidekick, Pup, plus my famous Dagwood sandwich, prepared while the folks were napping. The siblings had dispersed to parts unknown, leaving a young lad a free run at the kitchen, ice house and pantry! That's a triple play!

If there were desires I should have had, I confess I never noticed nor did I feel I missed anything worth while! The world was unfolding correctly today!

Older Bro had an adult lunch kit, the double buckle job with the rounded top that could hold a thermos bottle or, in my case, a large pop bottle. The lunch bucket was off limits to me by a country mile I had discovered on several occasions, but on a Sunday afternoon, Bro was out, likely chatting up some "birds," who knows!

The pop bottle fit neatly into the rounded, black top of the bucket, making the lunch kit somewhat top heavy for the moment, that is, till I thumped my Dagwood sandwich into the bottom compartment, making the bucket stand at perfect attention and balance. A few cookies tucked into the corners of the bucket prevented any tattletale rattling as I slithered out the back door of our house with my plunder.

Pup, being wise to the action he had observed through the screen door, was waiting and wagging his tail somewhat impatiently, but without moan or whimper. Pup just loved these excursions despite the fact that not a wholesome thought likely crossed his mind all afternoon, while my mind on the contrary was heavy with agenda!

So whether it was herding cows or a Sunday afternoon exploration trip, make that a trip where solitude would reign. I preferred to call it a "walk about."

I avoided the shortcut through the garden, as the folks open bedroom window might allow our plans to seep in, and this was known to wreck havoc with a young man's agenda! Through the pasture, but close to the safety of the fences as the bull was on duty this afternoon. Soon we cleared the danger zone without incident and the fields were now as open to our choices as the agenda was.

Pup always assumed I had deep thoughtful plans for the day, and never insisted on foisting any of his wishes upon me at this stage. In fact, until the lunch bucket was opened, Pup was devoid of any thoughts as far as I could tell. Wagging his tail and letting his long tongue hang out was about as much responsibility as he could muster.

The small bluff of maple trees at the far end of our property beckoned, as the soft breeze blew towards us. Pup was alerted to a jackrabbit in small brush along the fence line. The chase was on, both the jackrabbit and me were aware of who the winner of the chase would be. The chase was short lived, as was Pup's breath, and he returned to me with his tail wagging, as if he had indeed taught the rascal a lesson.

I patted pup on his head and fluffy tan coat of hair remembering just in time that Pup always was pleased with my slingshot aim, despite the many misses! He was sure he had atoned himself well with me, remaining alert in case another rabbit was to be given a light workout!

The hollow, just outside the bluff, was on a slight knoll. The wind had not discovered this location as I lay down on the grassy slope.

Pup was eyeing the location of the lunch bucket, but Mom's Sunday lunch was being digested in my tummy and Pup would have to wait, till I, too, was hungry. Then too, Pup was tired from his mighty chase of the jack and needed to rest and regenerate energy for the return trip and any emergencies he might have to address. I laid my large straw hat over my eyes, and Pup knew I was addressing the burgeoning thoughts that the universe was expecting me to give input to.

The sweaty smell of my straw hat did seem to inspire new thoughts, not all pleasant ones! I peaked out from underneath the sweaty dome to see whether Pup was relaxed, which he was, and now I could slide the aroma filled sun shield to the side without letting Pup know I was cheating. Pup was cuddled at my side, eyes closed in meditation, or something to that effect. He was no threat to disturbing my subject matter.

First off was that huge blue sky. I rolled my eyes from side to side to try to make a better estimation as to its height and breadth. Soon as I was "grown-up," I would make a point of flying up real high in an airplane, then I could see what Heaven really looked like! God loved young boys, my Sunday school teacher Anna had assured me, and so I was quite confident that I would be welcome for a look-see; after all, I wanted to be a full time resident of Heaven some day! Pictures taken by Dad's camera fascinated me and while I was flying I would sneak up and take a close up picture of the horizon! This, to my considerable knowledge, had not been done yet and would certainly make the newspaper headlines! "Young herdsman talks with God and snaps a close up shot of the horizon on his return trip!" Yes, I liked that! This thought so pleased me that I must have squirmed a tad, and Pup took advantage of my open eyes and nudged the lunch bucket with his long nose. I failed to catch the hint and he, like me, dozed off again.

A thought that I had invested considerable time in was again to be reviewed and hopefully advanced to its fruition soon. Even as a young lad, I had my own Credit Union bank account. I was still not clear on the purpose of the decimal point. When I read my little Credit Union booklet stating the amount of my considerable funds, I became confused whether the amount to my credit was $5.00, $50.00 or $500.00 dollars.

I felt certain that whatever the amount was, it was a hefty sum. After all, details were not for me to deal with. In fact, I had overheard a businessman in town say that "the devil is always in the details."

This had, and still was giving me the bejibbers, as Anna, my Sunday school teacher, had nothing good to say about the devil! So onward with my game plan that would surely rock the financial world. My secret plan was to withdraw some funds from my account and slowly but systematically buy up the coinage in all of Canada! Sure, I would start small, buy the pennies as they became available, and move to the nickels and dimes as my venture grew. The words *blackmail, ransom,* and *hoarding* were not in my vocabulary at the time; *profit* was! After I had cornered the penny market, the business world would be begging at my doorstep. Unreasonable I would not be, and would offer the penny stash back into the market, but at two cents for each penny! After all, what choice did the world have except to pay my asking price? I had a monopoly! The plan sounded solid enough to me, but the timing was not right and so I put the idea back in a holding pattern, to be reviewed when the conditions seemed more appropriate, as I had done many times already.

In later years, I laughed when I read how the Hunt Brothers in Texas tried a somewhat similar venture with the silver market. Their plan, like mine, never did succeed!

I had another urgent thought, but had to put the idea on hold as Pup now put his large paw, complete with claws, on my chest. Pup did remain friendly as his tongue hung out, and was dripping saliva on my Sunday shirt. Pup won the day and I sat up, reached for the lunch kit. Pup had put a claw mark on Big Bro's lunch bucket and this might call for an explanation if I was discovered to have hijacked the slick looking status symbol.

Pup insisted on sniffing the contents in the lunch bucket. In order to get his saliva- dripping tongue away from the sandwich, I sacrificed a cookie. This gave me a chance to relocate the bucket while he was busy chewing the small morsel. I closed the bucket and invited Pup to join me as I headed to the fence with my pop bottle in hand. I had learned to remove the bottle cap with almost any metal object. A hammer edge, a screwdriver tip or even the hasp in the fence post. The cap popped off as expected and a long, satisfying slug of the fizzy liquid, it felt refreshing. My plans, I had rerun and restored, but it had taken its toll on my digestive system and was now both hungry and thirsty. Pup may well have saved me from starvation, as I had been in my thought trance. The Dagwood sandwich was shared on an unequal basis, but Pup accepted that he would be ripped off a tad. Pup lapped pop from my cupped palm hand.

Predictably his eyes went crossed, and a mighty sneeze was released. I had cleared the area in advance as pup released a double blast and then pawed his considerable snout. This done, he ran to me with tail waving, hoping for a repeat of the thirst quenching liquid.

Bucket and bottle now both depleted, I lay back in the hollow, trusting Pup would allow me another session of my thought-provoking plans. In fact, it was not really a plan I needed to apply my brain trust to, it was a theory or something close to that. During the week, a fine rain had been granted us. Our summer kitchen was some fifty feet from our house and connected by a concrete sidewalk. During the height of the rainstorm, both Dad and myself were called to the summer kitchen. Dad ran the fifty feet from the house to the kitchen, while I chose to prove my recently developed theory that running in a rain storm did not keep you dryer than walking did. Dad, who for the most part was dry, listened to me as I stood there dripping wet, explaining my newly developed hypothesis. The fact that Dad had run and was dry, and I had walked and was wet, did not lessen my convictions any! Dad listened, seeing my enthused explanation, reluctantly agreed—softly even—but had that smirk on his face that had in the past suggested I do more work on this subject I was attempting to advance!

My theory was thus: Dad had run in the rain, and therefor had received raindrops on him that he would not have encountered had he walked. The raindrops would have fallen harmlessly in front of him to the ground, but in his "foolish running," he had now been struck with these drops.

I again, in my youthful wisdom, had walked! So those raindrops had fallen to the ground in front of me and not struck me as they had done to Dad while he was rushing. Dad, not wanting to stifle thought, agreed that I might have a "breakthrough" with my theory but encouraged me to give the theory some more workouts before declaring my revelation to the general public.

The cows were on the back forty acres now and soon it would be milking time. In case I should be seen returning with my loaned lunch bucket, I thought it wise to bring the cows on my return trip. I stayed next to the fences and sent Pup out to do the dirty work of moving cows and bull to the barnyard.

I was still perplexed as to why Dad had not whole-heartedly declared my rain theory a breakthrough of considerable proportion. I don't recall where or when I added "time" to my rain theory that only contained distance and speed but I never again advanced this thesis to Dad and mercifully, neither did he.

The afternoon had been a good investment I decided. I felt good about the solitude I had enjoyed. The lunch bucket was not missed and the scratch on the lunch bucket never made news! Mom was pleased that I was satisfied with a "light Sunday brunch"! As for Pup, he laid down under the porch, business as usual.

Mennonite Motorcycle Mania

Most of Mom's siblings, fifteen of sixteen, lived in an area of Southern Manitoba—primarily in the Rocky Mountain area—south of the town of Morden. Our farm where I grew up was a massive twenty miles from the main clan's digs.

Mom's oldest sister lived in "never-never land" called Vancouver, BC, or so it seemed that it was a world away. Whenever my Aunt Helen or my cousins from Vancouver did come to southern Manitoba for a visit, it was a huge occasion!

So it was on this one Sunday that my cousin Benny had come to touch base with his roots. The bigger story and cause for excitement was that Benny had arrived on a motorcycle! At this time, motorcycles were quite rare, and to have driven from Vancouver to southern Manitoba on one made him a work of art! A sighting of a motorcycle was cause for great excitement at this time in my life!

Benny was a handsome dude! Nearly six feet tall, a washboard rib cage, that you could see through his t-shirt. Big Harley belt buckle (to die for when you are a kid), and blue jeans, tight where they should be!

For me, meeting my cousin for the first time, I will admit, was overshadowed by the fact that I was going to see a motorcycle up close, touch it, likely get to sit on the idle machine as it leaned lazily on its kick stand. To an eleven-year-old lad, to have sat on a motorcycle, even an idle one, would certainly be a story for school in the fall! An entire recess would be filled with relating the action-packed experience!

Sunday afternoon finally arrived, as did our family on Grandpa Zacharias farmyard. The large farmyard was located on a modest-sized hill, with the rocky driveway leading past the huge garden and new monster red barn. A lightning strike had burned the original barn a few years back. The driveway had all the elements of rock, some shale, gravel and real big rocks that only had a bald head sticking out.

Our family had a reputation of arriving early, then also leaving early so as to get those precious chores done on time back on that twenty-mile-away farm job, on Flatfields! Mom was not programmed, it's just that she wrote out her diary a day ahead of time! Further to that, my mom had no eraser on her diary pencil, so getting it right the first time was her goal, okay—obsession!

So early we were, which augured well for me! The shined blue Harley was sitting in a protective area near the front door of the older, but well-kept, Granny's house. I wasted no time with going inside the house and "doing any niceties" such as meeting Cousin Benny. I headed straight for the coveted motorized two-wheeler. It did not disappoint! The nubby tires, the leather seat, two saddlebags—although smaller size. The kick starter pedal that could make this metal beast spring to life was intriguing to me. My mind was racing along with this machine, the wind even had little chance to react to my action!

More uncles, aunts and scores of cousins were now arriving, which did not bode well for me to ask Benny a few questions I feared. My cousins and myself were milling about the admired machine when a tall, lanky young man stepped into the fray, "I am Cousin Benny," he said. No one else bothered to mention their name, there were too many to remember at any rate. Harley was spoken here!

Benny tossed his long slender leg over the Harley seat, threw a switch, one kick-start and the machine, as expected, roared to life! The circle of cousins just backed away a few feet, as the machine snorted in the mandatory warm-up! The noise of the snorting warm-up enlarged the crowd to include uncles and aunts.

Looking directly at me, since I had forgotten to back off from the vibrating noise, Benny asked, "Are you ready?" Faster than a dog at a fire hydrant, I had my leg up and over the seat with a bit of assistance by grabbing Benny's broad belt that had a huge belt buckle that said Harley on it. "Hang on," I heard Benny shout and, with a half-donut cut, we were underway!

I squeezed Benny's washboard waist tight, sure I had dreamed that I might sit on the stationary machine, but to actually have a ride on the bike—this was over the top for me! My mind was trying to savour the moment and yet keep up to the fast action! Down the rocky driveway we roared, gravel just spitting aside from the tires, meeting more cousins coming to see Benny, or the bike, or both. Hanging on to Benny was more important than a wave at my cousins, although I would have liked to gesture, just to let them know it's me on this whiz machine! At the end of the long driveway, I expected Benny to cut another half-donut and return to the farmyard—wrong!

Down the hilly dirt road we went, the wind whistling through my hair and making my eyes water-blurry. I peeked around Benny's waist and saw the speedometer sitting at fifty-plus miles an hour! Never, ever, nowhere had I gone fifty miles per hour! The neighbour's dog had come to the road with the honourable intention of wetting the mailbox pole, as he did every day. Leg in the air, the sight of something moving this fast caused the dog to forget what his mission had been! A gopher scampered across the road, just barely missing the whirring front wheel of the Harley! The gopher would need to sharpen up on his timing if he were to exist past this afternoon! Benny slowed the machine at the next intersection of the all-clay road. A gentle U-turn, with Benny's shoe scraping the dirt a bit, then Benny gunned the machine to again what seemed to be like the speed of light!

The, narrowly missed gopher had now requested a witness to see the near disaster he had encountered. Two gophers, standing a full foot tall, were on the side of the road. Not a blink of a beady eye from the two, only the necks craned with us as we blurred by them! The dog, still petrified or frozen in time, was still debating whether to stick with his original mission of wetting the pole or to go yelping back to his master's yard and cower under the porch! A quick glance behind me showed he choose the third, unplanned option, gently lowered his leg and headed home, the pole marking could be done at a later, slower-paced day!

Up the rocky driveway, past the red barn, to a cheering group of relatives! Off the bike I jumped, with a grinning Benny asking my name. "John" I stammered, still trying to get my dry tongue to work! "Saw you admiring the machine," Benny said. "Wanted to see if your guts matched your enthusiasm," he mused. "You don't scare easy, do you?" cousin said, as he beckoned another cousin to get on the seat behind him. My day was complete! I held the land-speed record in my family! The other, more timid, cousins crowded round me, my first news scrum kind-of, asking how it was and should they dare try it if Benny asked them. "Certainly it's not for the faint of heart, we were doing close to sixty," (the speed had increased slightly since the ride), "Keep your legs in and a tight grip on Benny," was my advice, lacking no confidence at the moment was I!

I could now hardly wait for school to commence, with a story like this to tell! The speed we had traveled at was now a confirmed sixty—sounded like a nicer number too!

All the way back to our farm, I reminded Dad that he was only doing thirty-five miles per hour, while I had gone almost twice that on the motorcycle! The entire family breathed a sigh of relief when we arrived home, while I was in fine fettle, quite prepared to do another re-run of the day's events!

Benny had an un-eventful trip back to BC. Some fifty years later, I again met Benny and to my dismay Benny could not recall the highlight ride he had given me. He recalled coming to Manitoba on the bike, but the lifelong thrill he had given me was, like the ride, in the past! I had enough memories of the ride for both of us!

Home after the house/barn divorce, 1948.

Lock-less House on the Prairie

Having no locks or keys for your house doors may sound just a tad unbelievable in today's world, yet that was the world I was born into back on our little farm. Yes, summer, winter, spring and fall, our house doors were unlocked or, better said, they had no locks in most cases.

I never did discuss such mundane issues with my school pals as whether their doors had the luxury of a lock, it was a non-event with me. In fact, I would be surprised to hear that any of the neighbours would have had locks and keys on their properties. The 300 gallon fuel tanks farms all had were unlocked! Keys were left in the ignition of all your vehicles, which was a Model 1936 four door sedan at that time. Farm homes were not locked when the family was away.

Without phones at the time, it was not uncommon to arrive at a relative's farmyard and find they had also gone visiting. It was customary, while silly, to leave your "mark" on the farm, informing your friends that they had visitors call while they had been away.

I cannot recall that our family ever entered another person's home when they were not at home. Many families thought little of doing just that when they went to visit another family (no phones on the farms) and the people were away. They would enter the other family's home, perhaps put chairs on the tables, etc., as a prank and a guessing sign that someone had come to visit them. I realize this sounds somewhat bizarre, but we were plain farm folks that were a happy lot. The dining room table had an oilcloth on it, no scratch problem! Should be noted that many families had only chairs for the parents, with the kids sitting on wooden apple crates turned on end.

No note was left, at least no name, so the owners of the house, upon their return home, had to guess as to who had paid them a visit. Again, at times it was hours and days in spare moments we pondered and wondered who could have been at our house. Today, parties are thrown with the murder-mystery as entertainment. Way back when, this was our form of visitor mystery—that bit of 007 in all of us!

Yes, at times one could tell who had been at our house to visit us by the type of pranks they would leave behind. Tire car tracks were traced, Dick Tracy style; were they wide or narrow tires? Pranksters have a tendency to repeat the same type of prank each visit. It became somewhat of a trademark, when a certain prank was left, you knew whom it had been that paid you a visit. Other families chose to leave a different mark each visit so as to throw you off the track and keep you wondering. Rarely, but it has happened where we had not figured out who had been at our house until we met again with these folks and they would reveal that it was their family. This would, of course, involve a lot of teasing and ribbing with such a "gotcha"! Other times our neighbours, having seen the car come and go on our yard, the vehicle description was a great help in our family investigation, thus blowing our jokester guest's cover. Of course, we did not admit to the neighbour's help in our "little gumshoe" probe, but it sure confounded our guests, when we later met them, as to how we foiled their plans. Great fun it was!

My parents did not enter another person's home when the people were away, but it was common to take and pile items that looked handy in front of the house door. Items like farm pails, perhaps a ladder, anything that would obstruct and be easily noticed. Dad was super careful to never cause damage to anyone's property. At some homes, the family dog was very protective and would not allow us to come near the master's front door. We did respect both the dog and the owners by not coming up to the house. At one of my uncle's house we piled items in front of his door with his dog present, but not objecting to our presence. To our amazement, next time we met, my uncle laughed in our face, knowing we had done the prank. Perplexed we were how he was so sure we had been to their house. His smiling response, "Remember the dog you gave us some years ago?" Without waiting for an answer, Unc continued. "No visitors," he said, "Get past the gate when we are not home. The dog still remembered you as his master, therefore allowing you in." Dogs have long, fond memories"!

Most homes had a protective fence around their house. The protection was from their own cattle as often the animals roamed loose on the farmyard. The dog or dogs would allow us up to the front gate, thus that gate became the target for pranks. The capers were for the most part "fun pranks" with no damage done. They became a laughing item next time the parties involved met. In hindsight, it strikes me as somewhat crass to play such little tricks, but at the time they provided a good laugh for all. We must remember, this was Hill-Billy country and we too had some of that blood coursing through our veins!

As the adage goes: You don't stop laughing when you get old, you get old when you stop laughing!

I can recall being able to go along to town and was fascinated by the large locks that the various merchants had on their doors.

One particular store lock caught my fancy, as the keyhole was at least 2 inches tall and quite wide. I did see the key for the lock and it was a monster of a key. Half a foot long and one knobby affair at the end, not the fancy cut keys that came along later; certainly this one would not fit in a pocket.

Most every town and hamlet had a night watchman and it was his duty to check all the doors of the business front doors. After that, he walked the back alleys checking those doors as well. At times when the merchant came in the morning, he would find a note on his desk from the night watch man saying, "I found your door open." If the note said "again," that was a minor warning that the merchant was a bit sloppy with locking up. When the note read "this is the third time this month I found your door unlocked," that could net the merchant a visit from the town policeman, which, at times, was the same guy as the night watchman. While most such visits were done with a smile, it was nevertheless recorded at town hall that the merchant had been visited and for what reason. Should a merchant then report a robbery, it would be looked upon with a jauntiest eye. The insurance company might be somewhat balky at paying a claim.

We began locking our doors on the farm when I was about ten years old. We had noticed suspicious things happening in our house. More on that a bit later.

Gradually this locking of doors turned into a firm policy and was partially because a neighbour had all his pork smoked hams pinched on him one late fall, snowstorm night. The neighbour had a good-sized family. He therefore had a pig-killing bee, slaughtered four large sows each fall. The hams (hindquarters) were kept intact, were then stuffed with salt, plus heavily smoked in a special smokehouse. The farmer had completed this process, was likely proud that he had "looked after his family" with a winter and spring supply of meat.

On this occasion, the speculation was that "at least two too many ears" had heard the comments about the meat all smoked and packed in his salt barrels in the winter shed. At the local store that doubled as a gossip shop, these pig-killing bees, plus the work involved, were well verbalized. A few days hence, an early but fierce snowstorm hit! The sharp-eared and nimble-fingered thief struck when the winds were howling and visibility was near zero. Mother Nature covered his tracks perfectly, with the wind muffling any noises the thief might make, even making the guard dog take a night off due to the storm. The farmer was snuggled in bed while the thief was "looking after his winter supply of pork." In the "good ol' days," the police were seldom called on such matters. The rumor mill for the most part was the "judge and jury"! Kids, being kids, were rather pleased about "Daddy supplying their winter's meats" and spoke about such matters in school. While the parents hearing these stories, knew that no pig killing had taken place at that "certain neighbour," in fact that farmer had no hogs, it became rather clear where those hams had come from. The light-fingered neighbour was a very poor farmer with a large family. The other "victim farmer," well to do, did not pursue the matter as the sticky-fingered guy paid the price by not having the courage to attend those impromptu men's meetings at the local little store. These stories, as they made their rounds from person to person, were the reasons that door locks became the norm on many farms.

In our case, one reason that locks became into play was when we became suspicious, after one of my siblings noticed that "an item in her room" had been moved from windowsill to her dresser. Since we as a family, for the most part, respected each other's space, the question went out, "Who had been in her room?" When all the siblings and parents pleaded "not guilty," our minds went into overdrive as to who might be taking an un-invited interest in our property, sparse as it was!

The instances of items being moved went to other rooms of our house in subsequent weeks, then a few items, such as trinkets, went missing that were keepsakes. It was noted that all these instances had happened on Sunday morning, when our family was in church. We had a hunch, but wanted to be certain.

Having recently brought our house locks into working shape, we decided it was time to lock our house doors confident we had now turned the tide in our favour.

Next Sunday, again, after church we found someone had moved some items about. We were puzzled, locked doors, yet someone had been inside our house! Our collie dog Pup was acting somewhat strange by running about our back porch and basement door, which we choose not to place much credence.

Mennonites, not believing of ghosts past or present, were not beyond a "gumshoe" program!

Our house was locked, except, one family member noticed one small, back door that led to the basement was not lockable. Then, of course, the entire house became open to the intruder. We corrected that shortcoming in our security program by installing several hooks on the door from the inside.

It was time to enact a plan.

Next Sunday morning, our car roared off the yard to church as per normal, minus my dad, who would watch the action, if any, and hopefully solve the mystery.

My Dad did not have a long wait that Sunday morning. After we left the yard, he peered through the curtained window towards our front yard. The suspected new neighbour, who had befriended our watchdog during his regular daytime "neighbourly visits" that were common on the farm, came walking through our yard with confidence. Dad later said, "It was easy to see that this routine was comfortable to the trespasser by now."

As he did his PR thing with our dog, he walked briskly towards the back door area of our house. Dad, seeing his path, opened the back door of the house just as the confidant Tim was walking past towards the basement door.

When Dad gave him a firm "good morning" while Tim was in full stride, Tim jumped back as if to run. Very startled and nervous, Tim attempted "small talk" but was unable to explain in clear words what his mission had been on our yard on a Sunday morning and heading for our basement door. The visit was short, never repeated—even his daytime visits during the weekdays did not happen anymore. Dad made no accusations of any kind, nor did he mention the missing items. Smaller items had vanished in the past but nothing of significance or great monetary value went missing and we closed the case on the matter without even a whisper in the neighbourhood. Such a release of info, even the fact that he was caught on our yard and items moved in the house, would have "blown" the neighbourhood relationship into fragmentation! For us, it was mission accomplished in that no further "visits" were noticed. Had he walked through our open farmyard to our garden, we would not have given the situation a thought. But to come walking into our home path, leading to our back door, that crossed the line! For our part, a lock was now on the small basement door as well and I guess that's how our small area's "innocence" was lost.

We as a family felt a loss, in that the neighbour did not feel comfortable paying us the neighbourly visits that all had enjoyed in the past.

No sooner had we become accustomed to locking our doors and feeling secure than along came an intrusive device called the "skeleton key." This was a long-handled key, looking as innocent as any other key of the day, but was the "master of keys"! It would unlock most any standard house door locks and most house door locks were the standard variety! The new key was available in many stores, for anyone's purchase.

At first it seemed like a handy key to have, one key fits all. Soon however abuse of this key was becoming apparent. The next security step was to install new locks on the house doors that had a new shaped key the skeleton key would not open. To save on costs, many farmers did as we did, entered and exited by only one door of the house when locking up, thus only one new lock was required. The other door's locks were disabled from the inside, with only the thumb bolt workable.

It was widely speculated that a lock company that knew sales of new locks would become brisk once the skeleton key dangers became known had mass manufactured the skeleton key. If that was the case, the lock company was right—new door locks were on many shopping lists.

Soon all the cars, trucks, tractors had starters and keys. Keys became items to be under rugs or on top of the house door-frame, or carried about in our pockets. Locksmiths did not exist in our part of the country at that time, duplicates were for the most part unheard of. That changed quickly as lock companies had key-cutting machines installed in hardware stores, duplicate keys became the norm.

Still, our one room Spears school remained unlocked 24 hours a day through the 8 grades I attended there. In fact, on one occasion the teacher did request a key from the trustees of the day, but were unable to produce one. While isolated thefts did occur, none of significance ever occurred in our area that I became aware of.

Dog-gone Olympics

Our collie dog, "Pup," was not your ordinary dog. He not only loved to play the standard fetch games, but he invented some games on his own.

His enamel food bowl, three inches deep and ten inches across, was found turned upside down for no apparent reason. Pup put his nose to the side of the bowl, pushing it around the yard. Soon his nose-bowl centre dexterity became so efficient, that Pup was able to chase all around the farmyard at full dog speed, rarely losing the bowl, which, if it did happen, only caused a quick restart! Should the bowl, when it hit a bump, flip open side up, one well-placed paw on the side of the bowl would reverse the bowl, allowing the fast game to continue. Finally, with tongue hanging out, some laps of cold water, and Pup was ready for any other action we could offer.

Playing hide and seek was a big favourite of all the family, with Pup leading the way! We would throw a soft rubber ball as far as our arms would allow. Pup would fetch the ball during which time we would hide. The ball now back and dropped, he would, in very short order, with his keen sense of smell locate us where we felt we were well hidden. Again, with practice, our hiding locations became more difficult for Pup to find us, we felt, but he ratcheted up his hi-tech nose and discovered our devious hiding spots with ease.

As family, we put our heads together to try to outsmart him in locating us. The barn hayloft could be accessed via vertical, wooden slats on the inside barn wall. A top-hinged lid was lifted to gain access to the hayloft. Pup was not aware of the plot being hatched by the family against him! The loft lid was propped open with a stick for quick access well ahead of game time. After several usual warm-up hiding locations, while Mom and Dad were watching, we decided the time had come for the big planned rout to be given a try.

Dad was given the task of giving the ball the longest heave-ho he could deliver, giving us kids a bit more time to scramble up the vertical ladder. Mom and Dad positioned themselves so they could observe the anticipated action, expecting Pup to lose this round. The long ball was fired, with the kids, like scared monkeys, chased up the ladder and closed the lid with a kick on the stick prop. All were silent. Pup returned and went through a few of his easier search routines, unaware that his skills would be thoroughly tested this time. A few incorrect locations checked by Pup, the parents reported. His brain twigged that something new was happening. His long, pointy nose was twitching while turned up in the air. In a split second, Pup was at the base of the barn ladder, barking in frustration that he was not able to pounce on us as he enjoyed doing! We were again clearly beat! On the rare occasion that he tired of the game sooner than us kids, he would not chase the tossed ball but be right on our heels as we attempted to hide. A big wrestling match would ensue, with a resting truce declared and welcomed by all.

On occasion when the family was gathered outside after a hard day's work, Big Bro would tease Pup by giving him a square of toffee. Pup had a sweet tooth and could not refuse the bait. The toffee would stick to Pup's teeth and gums. The contortions Pup's mouth went into was laughable but borderline shabby!

Pup, however, was always game for a second toffee, totally disregarding the chicanery he had just experienced. Pup craved attention and he had ours!

Pup's skill at fetching the cows from the far reaches of the pasture near milking time, were very helpful. Pups style was however a bit too aggressive to be allowed completely on his own. Yes, he would enjoy bringing the cows home all right, however the pace he set was in excess of what good milk production practices permitted. With one of the family in voice reach of Pup, the pace was slower but more appreciated by cows and milking personnel alike.

In spring or fall when the cattle were free-ranging, the bovines could be several miles away from our farmyard when milking time was nearing. A climb onto the barn roof with the handy binocs, we could locate where the errant cows had found the grass greener that day.

A saddle on the old grey mare, Pup always ready to join me in the "cow hunt," never to complain about distance. The job needed to be done, and you could count on Pup! A stray free-range bull would on occasion join our herd when the bull felt the "pickins" might be worthwhile in our herd. Pup was quick to recognize the strange animal, with the bull soon aware that "retreating was the better part of valour."

In his latter years, a lightning strike on our farmyard scared Pup so that he sought shelter underneath a visitors car. Unaware of Pup's hiding place, Pup was run over by the car. That situation repeated itself several times in future lightning storms.

While Pup was a tough critter, the damage from these run overs did manifest itself with arthritis in his hindquarters, causing a lot of pain for him.

Pup was protective of his master and master's property as well. He was not vicious, but snarly as well as nippy on stranger's heels. He put on a good show when strangers arrived but turned watchdog when the family had vacated the farmyard. Many a cream can full of that revenue-bearing matter was not picked up when we had not been at home when the cream pick up schedule had been altered without our knowledge.

Mr. Bergen, our closest neighbour, frequented our farm often, had, for reasons unclear to us, made up his mind to have a running battle with Pup each time he paid us a visit. The neighbour's poke of his cane was a real irritant to Pup. On one occasion that I witnessed, the neighbour was just entering our home via the back door. The steps conquered, the aged neighbour could not resist that quick rap of his cane on Pup's nose before entering the already-open screen door. Pup could not resist either! Grabbing the fellow's heel firmly with his adequate mouth, the neighbour found himself on all fours at the bottom of the stairs once more! Pup did a hasty retreat, as he knew he had responded out of character as well as the masters wishes.

The visitor was unharmed and in future visits only stares were exchanged, with the feeling remaining mutual between dog and visitor!

The reason for the neighbour's animosity, we speculated, was that Pup was a bright, good-looking dog, where as the neighbour's dog was a barking coward and ugly mongrel to boot! Horses, dogs were all part of a pride the farmers had for their animals.

The "medicine peddlers" that trolled the farmhouse wives with their overpriced merchandise were a favorite target for Pup. When Mom was not keen on a peddler visit, she would not ask Pup to restrain himself. He knew he was "King Kong" in these situations, circling the peddler's car, wetting each wheel—twice if his "wet" supply permitted. From a rolled-down window of the car was a poor setting for the peddler to make a grand spiel of his wares, resulting in the peddler moving on. Those peddlers that were mildly welcomed by Mom, Pup was asked to oblige, which he reluctantly did. Even then, many a peddler was seen to back towards our house door clutching his suitcase of snake oil and pleading with Pup to heed his master's instructions. The smarter peddler learned to have a bag of cookies, (stale ones no doubt) in the car. One or two cookies did lessen the growling, but a sigh of relief was heard or was visible each time the peddler was safely indoors! When Dad was at home, Pup was much more reserved, but in his absence, he was there to protect "the hand that fed him everyday"!

While Pup did not have to remind Dad of his value to the farm, he did what he felt was required in a given situation. It was a Sunday afternoon, Mom and Dad had an event to attend that would not permit them to be part of the farm chores that evening. Our big, black Angus bull had been released that morning when it was deemed that one of the lady bovines might appreciate his attention.

Dad was not however comfortable leaving us kids to handle the bull when it was time for the cows to enter the barn for milking. So, Dad decided to have big Angus come in at noon. Angus, while having his one date completed, had sensed another heifer throwing off interesting vibes to him. Dad knew this date was "for tomorrow," Angus wanted to make this a "two goal" day and resented the early call to the barn.

Bro and Dad entered the pasture to seek out the Angus for the barn call. The Angus suddenly turned on both men, knocking Dad to the ground with his large but hornless head. The bull continued to maul Dad as he lay helpless on the ground. The Angus straddling Dad with his front feet, while jamming his head into his chest and stomach area. Bro beat the bull with a stick, which proved fruitless.

I was sitting or kneeling safely on the ground on the other side of the fence, terrified! Pup was circling the action, seemingly confused as to how to help. I hollered "Sic, sic!" meaning go get him! Now Pup sprang into action, biting the bull's hind legs viciously. While this distracted the bull, he was determined to do more damage to Dad. Pup had more ideas in his arsenal of tricks. With my yelling encouragement to Pup from a safe distance on the other side of the fence, he took a nice bite to the bull's "privates" that were hanging there for the taking! Without hesitation the bull backed away and was then so subdued that he headed for the barn!

Now in his stanchion, Angus received some sharp cracks from Dad's rarely used whip.

Next day, Angus was on the cattle buyer's truck, likely receiving the bologna award well ahead of his time.

Pup was again the toast of the farm! He appeared confused with all the praise and pats he was showered with by family members. All he had done, he felt, was what the situation had called for—protecting his master!

All in a day's work, Pup seemed to say as he made his rounds amongst family members, accepting every ear and head rub with his tail wagging in humble fashion. Dad was bruised but attended the function that was on their plate for that day.

Without Pup's help, we all doubted that the outcome would have favourable to Dad!

Flirty Dancing

Rabbits, in my eyes, are one of the more beautiful creatures God created in the animal world!

Rabbits, of course, have received a bad rap with common expressions such as *"Breed like rabbits," "Multiply like rabbits," "Horny as a rabbit."* Milder ones include *"Run like a rabbit"* or *"Eat like a rabbit."* There are several more adages that come to mind. Since these have only been overheard when the "second best human gender" has gathered and the male hormones are overflowing its bedroom banks. These aphorisms, were they on the stock market, would be classified as "speculative buys"!

As per norm there is some truth in all of these proverbs or dictums. Jackrabbits—well, they do multiply with 2-3 babies being common.

The cage variety of rabbit is likely the source of most of the adages, as these, I understand, are more prolific than the jacks in the wild.

Jackrabbits with its thick white winter coat of fine hair, the big buggy black eyes, a nose that's never satisfied or still! The spring-loaded hind legs give the jack those quantum fifteen foot leaps in full stride, yet appear to constructed for sitting up tall. Those elongated ears twist and turn like a TV satellite dish, giving the jack the ability to be totally appraised of all happenings about him! The powder puff tail is really as valuable as is a spoiler on the rear trunk of a cool dude's car, it's pretty but has little effect on the performance of car or rabbit! Add on the lighting fast ninety degree angles the jack can make in full stride, gives one a clue why many a fox has gone hungry!

My opportunity to observe these beautiful creatures being themselves came about one night when the age meter on me read twelve or thereabouts. While running the one horse sled for some hay bales in the far reaches of our farm yard one cold January day, I noticed, on the fence high snow banks, jack footprints in the new fallen dusting of snow. In fact, the snow bank had been trampled with rabbit tracks in an area the size of a barn. Hunting here at night would be akin to shooting ducks in barrel, was my initial reaction.

The hay bail stack was within twenty-five feet of the foot print area, making the perfect decoy for my anticipated target practice on the jacks that night. Several well placed hay bales and the black tarp that draped over the bales hung down just far enough to create the perfect enticement. A quick, early supper, the short winter days ushered in darkness by 6 p.m., when the anticipated gathering of jacks was likely to occur I deduced.

My favorite companion, Pup, found it difficult to understand why he was not permitted to join the party as I locked him in the barn.

With my .22 rifle loaded, I crunched my way over the hard snowdrifts hoping I was not too late and scare my intended prey. In the bright prairie moonlight, a ten-minute wait, the first jack came hopping calmly into view, not more than thirty feet away from my hay bale lair.

Before I was able to cock my loaded rifle, another jack appeared, than another and several more! My trigger finger became numb, my eyes not blinking! This was a sight few had ever witnessed, I felt certain!

The jacks were totally without fear, as the changes I had made with the hay bales were quite normal for them to expect as we hauled away hay bales near daily. Their white fur coats glistened in the full moonlight, with the black inside of the long ears in the alert position but not for the reasons I had seen in the past.

I soon realized I was in the process of crashing a very special Jackrabbit party, the annual spring mating dance! With jacks, one cannot tell the difference between male and female, somewhat by the size of the furry mammal, however with the furious activity, I had no choice but to trust the jacks' judgement. The thumping of the long hind paws on the snow bank could be likened to a snare drum sound! The dancing round and round, then reverse, now a complete "double axle" in mid-air (borrowing a skating term), with a new pattern of spin and dance.

The mating act itself was so fast that it took me a few minutes to catch on that it was occurring! The adage "Wham, bang—thank you ma'am," also attributed to rabbits, must have been coined by someone having witnessed what I was seeing! Lets just say the adage is much longer than the "jack act" takes to complete! From my ringside seat, a hutch of eight jacks—whether it was four of each I can not say—the jacks seemed unconcerned about such a trivial matter.

Had to contain my snicker when the recently shared joke at school recess came to mind. The scene had also been a wild rabbit dance, with one male somewhat over indulging in the action, supposedly hopping from one rabbit to the next saying "Wham, bam, thank you ma'am," till he became careless with checking the gender he was mounting and quickly asked, "Is that you Sam?"

Leaning over the hay bales on such a bright night, zero wind factor, whatever cold there was did not affect me or the jacks. I reminded myself several times that my mission tonight had been hunting the jacks! Shooting ducks in a barrel had been on my mind!

My rifle had already been uncocked, leaning against the hay bales beside me before I recall making that decision. In the moonlight I checked my watch to discover that I had now stood or leaned motionless for over an hour!

In my awestruck mental state, I noticed the jacks slipping away in various directions. I could only assume that the jacks had curfews to adhere to, or the males were sapped and they too get sleepy after a workout! I remained in my semi-prone position for a few minutes, savouring the sight I had just witnessed!

Picking up my rifle, I emptied the gun chamber of the unspent shells, totally satisfied with my action of not firing a single bullet! A dead jackrabbit or two could have likely been mine that night and would have been easier to explain when I got back to the house, as the "mighty hunter" question required an answer from my siblings. A few cheap comments from the siblings, a couple dead jacks just paled in comparison to the memory I have retained for over half a century of what I was privileged to have been able to observe that night! Nature left to its elements is a thing of beauty!

In spring, later that same year, Pup and I were doing our restless walk about when Pup noticed a now gray-coated jack sitting a distance away. When the jack did not move despite Pup's advancing on her, I called Pup off the normal chase he would have enjoyed. The doe rabbit was in the final birthing stages. We respected her delicate state, watching from a safe distance as two little "bunny jacks" came into this world.

My mind of course wandered back and wondered, had I witnessed both the "Genesis and Revelation" of these two bunnies? This again took me back to my pro and con feeling about sport hunting. Had my uncles come upon a mating dance such as I witnessed, being the true hunters, a few jacks would likely have been blown away from the blasts of their guns.

I was grateful for my double mind set on hunting, being able to hunt but also being able to control that hunting urge when the larger picture calls for restraint but provides a lifelong beautiful memory.

Bull Feathers

A sultry Sunday afternoon in mid July, pushing 12 years old, somewhat bored at home and the parents announcing they are going to visit my Uncle Rocky and Aunt Minnie. The parents are strongly encouraging me to join them on this visit, as I have not seen my cousin Ron for some time. The encouragement for me to join the folks, had no doubt been the culmination of talks between my folks and my older siblings behind my back.

Sis wanted no part of me staying at home with her as in her opinion, I had a penchant for getting into a mess of some kind, she being the laid-back, boring type in my books. Yes, I felt strongly that adventures—if they did not happen to come along in timely fashion—yes they had to be created, generally with a nudge from my creative mind!

Cousin Ron was almost three years my senior, at that age a three year age difference can seem like a lot, often more so by the older person. That was the case here, Ron, on our last visit about a year ago, had already shown body language that he was really doing me a favour by sharing his valuable time with my immature mind set. Ron's two brothers were even older than Ron.

Secondly, Uncle Rocky had shown little appreciation for young lads, at least those were the vibes I got from him at our past encounters. Unc struck me as one of those guys that cannot remember ever being young! His idea of a lad behaving well was to sit and ponder his navel! Likely not correct, but so it seemed to me!

Furthermore, at the last visit Unc Rocky and Aunt Minnie paid a visit to our farm, minus Cousin Ron, I had by my actions really "dissed" Unc Rocky! Not that I had intended to do so, but I had forgotten rule number one with Unc, he is number one with all his animals, be it horses, cows, pigs, dogs or pigeons! In his mind, whatever he owned was the best! Had to agree with him, in most categories, he was correct!

In wrestling boredom on their last visit, I put on "a performance" with Pup as Dad and Unc were sitting outside in the shade. Turning Pup's water bowl upside down was the signal to Pup that it was showtime. Pup dazzled that day, with his pointy nose on the upside-down bowl he zoomed around the farmyard causing some free-range hens to scatter and squawk. Pup also was an excellent fielder as I batted balls to him. Very few touched mother earth before he returned the ball to me. I had hit a raw nerve with Unc, his dog was just a mutt! Unc had been bested, big time!

Later when I was to meet up with Unc's dog, he was not uno one, not two, or even in the top ten in my books, that's where the wheels came off between Unc and me I gathered. Unc's dog was as dumb as a sack of hammers! As long as Unc had seen no better, his dog was number one, but after the witnessed performance at our farm, Unc knew he had received a kick in the "ego department"!

I knew for today, the die had been cast. So without further fuss, I joined the folks heading for Rocky Mountain, Hill-Billy country, where my relatives lived and had for a lifetime. True Hill-Billies, gun rack in the back pickup window, bib overalls, but decent, hard working folk.

On a large farm, in true country style, was a large fairly new barn and an old house. In Mennonite rationale, a barn produced a living while a house you just lived in! Many other, older barns stood on the farmyard, a pig barn, chicken barn, plus numerous smaller grain bins scattered about on the sprawly, large yard. My cousin was gone for the afternoon; I accepted that as a mixed blessing!

I was invited to "come and sit" with Dad and Unc Rocky. While often that would have been well received by me, today I had a militant spirit in me! It would not accept such a dormant thought as sitting and listening to adults questioning the crops, weather, etc.

"I prefer to do a walk about," I said matter-of-factly, assuming it would have many conditions attached to this idea, or be nixed. To my surprise, the idea was well received by both Dad and Unc. This gave them freedom to discuss all those touchy issues that young ears were not to hone in on, but for me, I would go with the flow—I had that inner feeling I could have more excitement on my own!

Unc had me figured as one that might get into trouble of some kind and likely why he gave me that get lost look! The glint in my eye must have been showing! Unc was a smart man and had me figured correctly, I grudgingly admitted to myself a second time. You know the feeling when you have an adult that has your number correct, but does not care much for you as you see it? That does poke at a few new emotions!

Unc in his stern manner gave me a heads-up, with prize horse barns *verboten*, purebred cattle in pasture out of bounds, including a bull with a nasty disposition. In fact, Unc continued, the bull is normally in the barn, however a young heifer had shown interest in having a date with the bull; even the pasture was "off limits" for me! The list of "no-can-dos" was shorter than I had expected.

Unc failed to mention his pride and joy, two hundred or so pigeons that had the loft portion of the machine shed for their nesting and resting home. Beautiful birds they were, in fact, prime breeding stock that he sold as people came a long distance to buy his fine specimens. His lecture about his pigeons was still very fresh in my mind from our last visit. Observing the pigeons from a distance was about all I remember, receiving Unc's blessing! My planned walk about appeared to be a very limited one, if guidelines were followed! My intentions were noble!

Unc had some interesting "values" in his lifestyle. Old house, old furniture—in fact, it seemed that all things that Aunt Minnie was to be contented with was old and borderline dilapidated. She was not chaffing about her lot in life, she was a hillbilly herself!

On the other hand, Unc had the newest rifles and guns, costly purebred cattle, pigeons that flew into his open-windowed grain bins costing him a fortune to feed! These were not a problem to him! His prize horses had shiny black harnesses, with silver trim. Although the horses were sparingly used these days, the cost of maintaining this team, was not a factor in his budget. The hunting budget was open-ended, it appeared to me!

Aunt Minnie was a happy gal. She never even gave it a mention that an imbalance in priorities might be at play on their farm. The man of the house was not only a king, but also a big king! This was common in some Mennonite homes, although a diminishing trait in most Mennonite culture. However this was "redneck" country, where any new trends applied to the men, with women still on the old era status quo! Unc Rocky treated Aunt Minnie well, as a person!

Unc was a true hunter! While most of my Rocky Mountain unc's were hunters, none was more dedicated, more enthused, or nutty about hunting than Unc Rocky! His shiny guns were hung on the wall, some in the living room. One could hardly imagine that Aunt Minnie had insisted the rifles hang there.

When the "hunter rutting season" sets in, the female species are not part of the equation! That of course sets the human hunter apart, of all other "ruts." Neither snow, sleet nor rain can stop a hunting expedition each fall, when the season for big game hunting is permitted legally. He had shot all the stuffed, mounted deer heads hanging in Unc's living room, personally. Ask a question about any one of these "prize flea havens" and you lost an hour of your life listening. A lot of interesting stories, I will concede, but did not hack it with me today!

When home freezers came into vogue, all the wild deer meat was stored in the freezer. If Aunt Minnie insisted on having some frozen fruit in the freezer as well, another freezer was purchased.

In the latter years, hunting permits were required, and limit of number of deer taken in a hunt enforced!

In earlier days, while meaningless permits were legally required, many hunted without permits and shooting a buck or two out of the legal season was but a twitch of the eyebrow. Wild venison was on Unc's home menu all year and nearly every day. Each home had a special way of preparing the venison so the wild flavour was masked, at least to their taste buds. Soaking the wild meat in vinegar before frying or roasting seemed to be the most popular choice, by my tender-ear survey of hunters.

I always marveled that my aunts accepted the husbands hunting craze, with seldom a fuss. On rare occasion, the fact that her new dress purchase had been put on hold, pending a better grain price, but hunting and the buying of gun shells never suffered such a cruel delay. Regurgitating the hunting stories I heard would be a book on its own, so one story shall suffice. Unc Rocky, in his declining years, was bedridden and had convinced himself that his days were all but done.

A birthday came along in Unc's home. Several families converged on the house to help celebrate the occasion. Unc was totally horizontal in bed. Dad and other visitors sat at his bedside for the visit. Unc had his eyes closed while the conversation swirled around him. By chance, one of the visitors mentioned something about a deer hunting expedition of the past. Unc's eyelids fluttered, than his eyes popped open. Soon he added something to the deer hunt subject. More hunting talk and in minutes Unc was on his elbow, propping himself up to make better eye contact with the visitors. The deer hunt was relived and soon Unc was sitting on the edge of the bed and in full combative conversation about the past hunt he had been a part of. The part where he shot the *"herch"* (male deer or buck) was told with some gusto evident!

Aunt Minnie was amazed, since Unc had not sat up for quite some time. So entrenched was Unc's hunting blood coursing through his veins that his illness was all but forgotten for this adrenaline moment!

Back to today! Dad and Unc had now retired to the rather limited living room in the house. I recalled our visit from a year ago, it being a safe bet that little had changed. You entered the house through a crowded lean-to, which served as a cat, dog domain, as well any and all garden tools, joined by spare boots, overcoats and hunting get up.

The small kitchen allowed you passage into a dining/living room combo. The walls held a stuffed moose head, ditto an elk head, with deer heads as filler of what could have been open space! Wolf and fox rugs on the floor beside some rifles propped alongside a grandfather's clock that revealed the correct time, only twice per twenty-four hours! Unc was a hunter, or better put, hunting was Unc!

The lumpy couch was Dad's choice, and while Mom and Aunt Minnie found comfort in the general area of the men, the conversation would definitely be divided between the sexes. Unc and Aunt were happy people!

My walk about the yard was limited. A shortcut through the *verboten* horse barn confirmed that the horses were well tended to. With the fences on rule one, "not entering the horse barn," now trampled successfully, my adventure spirit took that as a good omen.

The pigeons, much as I attempted not to notice them, were everywhere! The large opening at the end of the pigeon loft, facing the house, was buzzing with activity. The cooing, the flying in and out the loft from adult pigeons, as well as this year's hatching, was a fascination to me! I observed the pigeons for some time. The nesting arrangement, the roosting, if any, were questions that began to deaden the warning in my mind not to check on the prize birds.

In walking around the back of the machine shed, I noticed a door to the loft that, while looking unused for many a year, was on hinges and had a swivel closing. A wooden ladder lay flat against the wall of the near grain bin "Nah, I shan't" said my better judgement!

I challenged my conscience, "Give me a better idea to pass the afternoon!" Since no better thought was forth coming, I did a walk around the shed, just to be sure the "coast was clear."

I knew the drill on these visits between Dad and Unc. First, a sit about in the house for a good hour, with a healthy gabfest between the two farmers, was the norm. Now came the farm tour for the men, which by my estimate was an hour away.

I vowed to take but a tiny peak into the pigeon loft after having opened the half-sized loft door ever so gently, convincing my conscience that all would be well; the pigeons might not even notice, I reasoned!

The ladder now leaned against the machine shed, pigeon loft wall. As planned, I moved with cat-like stealth up the ladder, the swivel lock moved aside. I gently pulled at the bottom of the door, where my fingers had purchased a bit of space in the older, paintless building. The unused door was stuck! As I tugged again, the door flew open, nearly knocking me off the ladder and all of the estimated two hundred pigeons out the other end of the loft! The air was filled with loose feathers, dust, and flapping wings!

The cooing, fluttering flying noises created a huge fuss! The dog barked, surely Unc and Dad would not be long in coming! Panic set in! If Unc saw me, I was dead!

I slammed the door shut, jumped the eight feet to the ground, pulled down the evidence-laden ladder and ran into the back garden! I hurdled over one four-foot wire sheep fence, then another, through a barbed four-strand fence into the pasture. I ducked behind a large oak tree to catch my breath! Chubby was not accustomed to such a serious workout! I heard the house door slam, with my unc's excited voice wondering out loud as to the cause of his prize flock of pigeons unprecedented exit from the loft!

I was several hundred yards away, well-camouflaged with fences, underbrush and rows of tall garden corn! The dog, as I had surmised, was too old and lazy to be my undoing. Unc walked about the yard, muttering, speculating as to the cause of the pigeon's sudden exodus from their safe loft. That I would be a suspect was a given! I was attempting not to provide the evidence required for a huge tongue-lashing at least, far worse crossed my mind!

Since the men were in the yard already, the farm tour was combined with my unc' keeping an eye out for any hint of the cause of the excitement. Once the men entered the horse barn, I gambled that there would be a few minutes of admiring the horses before they would again continue the tour through the pig barn, chickens, etc.

I took advantage of the given time, my only option being to go further into the back woods, then a big, hour-long trudge through the "back forty," coming up the driveway to the house, whistling the most innocent tune,that would come to me! "Whenever you pull a scam, do it well," came to mind!

Messing with Unc's pigeons, guns leaning on every wall, not a perceived friend of young lads, how many reasons must one have before one engages the run option!

Certainly this beats boredom, I thought as I advanced further into the pasture, now hidden from the farmyard. A tad more relaxed as I surmised I needed to cross the pasture at an open spot if my mental compass was correct, to get to the road that would complete my plan of innocent escape.

In my mad dash from the pigeon loft, I had utterly and completely forgotten about Unc's bull warning! About the midpoint of the open pasture, behind a bluff of shrubby trees, I heard a decided snort!

That snort sound was not a friendly "welcome to my space, buddy!" Whatever relaxation had set in now vanished! Now Unc's bull warning came to me in a flash! There he was, all two thousand pounds of him, protecting his herd of well-fed cattle! Outrunning a mad bull, you can only win if there are two people running and you are the faster runner! I was alone! Pawing and snorting was he, while I was, once again, consulting my options department!

A large tree, halfway between me and the raging bull seemed my best hope! As I dashed toward the tree, the bull did the same from the opposite direction. The bull stopped once, pawing the ground and snorting as if he felt I needed convincing that he was serious! I required no convincing and kept on running towards the tree and the bull! The bull now was closing distance from the opposite side!

The old mighty oak had not a branch till about six feet above the ground, but had a nice slope in the trunk near the bottom before he shot straight up! The slope was in my direction and favour!

The bend in the tree trunk was what saved me, as I scrambled up the two-feet thick oak trunk, totally devoid of the thought that I was wearing Sunday clothes! "A trampled, dead guy don't look no good, Sunday clothes or not," I reasoned for a split-second.

A heavy branch at the seven-feet level was reached just as the raging bull did the same at the base of the tree! My heart rate was on overdrive—the second time in the last hour! The bull circled the tree, stopping to paw the ground, bellowing and shaking his large head while streams of silky saliva emanated from mouth and nostrils, while sticking out a curled tongue, all in one package! His eyes were bulging as he stared at me, "Gosh," I thought, "We have not even met and already you are mad at me!" He pawed the ground some more, sending the dirt and grass scattering above his hefty shoulders!

Now safe, or as safe as you can be with a bull circling a few feet below your dangling legs leaving no way of escape for me! I began surveying the damage to body, spirit, and Sunday shoes and duds! A scraped shin was bleeding some, trousers had some oak mildew stains, which I wrongly surmised I could brush out later. My shoes, some buffing from my handkerchief would bring back the shine! My finger that made contact with the barb wire fence was also bleeding. The damage done was all explainable, that is, if I lived to explain it!

The cows were observing the proceedings but not partaking in the action. Mr. Bull knew it was showtime for him, impress the cows, I felt he did!

A squirrel many feet above my head was protesting my dropping by without an appointment in his homey oak tree! I assured the squirrel as best I could, that "I was nuts, not looking for some!" Had the bull not stopped just once to re-demonstrate his anger at me, the outcome could have been much different!

I was content for the moment to count my blessings on my semi-safe perch, catch my bearings and planning an uneventful, safe excursion, in my round about way, back to my unc's driveway of innocence!

The bull reorganized his priorities when he spotted his "date heifer," with his amorous thoughts now returning to the fore! Considering it "mission accomplished" with me up a tree, he decided it best to go back and hopefully do what bull's primary function is to be.

The lead cow, replete with clanging bell, now began the slow trek towards the barn area, some half mile away. I remained motionless as the herd of cattle and the bull were slowly moving past the tree I was a hostage on. The prize herd of cattle now safely past me in the tree, I decided it was time to make another move, hopefully a less eventful one!

Now my avenue of escape was clear, disappearing into the woods hoping my mental compass would not forsake me. Complaining, squawking birds, chattering squirrels, these I could ignore, but the creek that lay in my intended route I could not. I walked along the winding creek, until a narrowing and a fallen tree aided my dry crossing. With a somewhat diminished appreciation of nature, that adventurous spirit that only a few hours ago had been so dominant, had now been dominated!

As I climbed the deep ditch to the sought-after dusty road, I brushed off the trousers as best I could, the handkerchief did wonders to my shoes! After a short walk towards my unc's place, I heard a car approaching behind me. The squealing brakes warned me that the car was stopping. My cousin Ron threw open the door with the old "hop in" message. My bad breaks were behind me, I mentally calculated as we drove up Unc's driveway.

The "where were you" quiz began as we stepped into the house for a light snack. Cousin Ron was quick to answer where he had picked me up on the road. As quickly as the questions had begun about where I had been, they also subsided. Unc seemed satisfied that, for once, this "glint-eyed" lad had not been involved in the pigeon caper.

On our return trip home, in the back seat of the car I steered the conversation in the direction of the great garden Unc and Aunt had. Dad relayed the pigeon incident, which now ranked second to the bull caper in my mind. Having no info to add to Dad's story, the conversation died off, but not before Dad, somewhat smiling over the agitated Unc. "Unc' Rocky will keep an eye out for the reason for the disturbance," Dad offered. I weakly advanced the cat theory (cat amongst the pigeons), finding that it had already been ruled out by Unc.

In the silence that followed for the balance of the homeward run to our farm, I hashed, rehashed (in my mind only) the afternoon and how I had handled the situation with the pigeons. Certainly, my unc would not have blown me away with a gun, those were loose thoughts! But the tongue-lashing from him with Dad there, likely another rehash of the incident at the lunch table with now Mom and Aunt present. Thirdly, a long ride home was assured with a predictable topic, an equally predictable message!

Deciding to seal this event in my mind, it has been hidden for over fifty years now! It was handled quite well! I gave myself a high mark! No one got hurt, no damage was done, a heifer had a honeymoon an hour later than planned, I had a fantastic memory tucked away for posterity!

I turned into bed early that night, puzzling both my parents!

Johns of Steel

Whenever we went visiting to the Rocky Mountain area, where most of my many cousins lived, we had a good time! Not that it really amounted to great stories, for the most part, but just messing around and talking about the nasty things we could do, but did not, seemed to please my style. Run close to the line but not over it or, if over then just a bit that one could explain it away, if required. Whenever these same cousins came for a visit at our house, well, I really had little choice but to also show them that I could provide an exciting afternoon of sorts, after all, at ten years old, there are options!

In fact, I seemed to suffer from a burning urge to go one better than what they had shown me.

Since these exchanges had been going back and forth, visit-wise, the "excitement bar" raised each time at least a tad, it was getting tougher to be over-the-top. Add to that, we guys were growing older with each visit, which again called for some action that was somewhat more advanced.

This Sunday, the cousins were at our house. Now it was time for me to match whatever adventure they had last offered or better still, beat it! The visit came as a surprise to me with my quiver (of tricks) not entirely loaded with a full compliment of arrows as it ought to have been. I was churning thoughts in my mind!

Last visit I recalled all to well! We had sauntered into the unlocked Spears school on a Sunday afternoon. I thought the teacher was away, which turned out he was not! We did some marginally scientific experiments in the small lab, at school. We did have some fairly bold mixtures of chemicals going when, for whatever reason, one test tube decided to become a Bunsen burner. No sooner had we extinguished the fire in another non-scientific manner, when we heard the school door opening softly. A quick window check revealed the most dreaded, it was the teacher! In what could be described as a fast clean up job, we left the lab or workshop room as expediently as we could, the chemical odours, we were not in control of!

With only one exit to the old fire-trap school building, we had no choice but to pass by the waiting teacher on our way out. The fumes from the surprise Bunsen burner, despite our clean up, hung heavily in the one-room school air. The teacher looked upset, so I did not stop to introduce my cousins to him! This may have been taken as disrespectful of me and could be why he appeared upset, judging by his facial expressions. Then again, causing the teacher to walk to the school from his abode, a full 100 yards away, was straining by his ambitions standard, so that may have also effected his attitude—especially on his day off! The fact that my cousins and me were interested in science on the weekend seemed to be overlooked!

So, today I stroked off any adventurous thoughts that lead in the direction of the school. I headed in the opposite direction and we were walking through our pasture towards the dugout, where the frogs could be tormented, and they were but that ranked as a so-so thing to do. While this kept my cousins busy, my young mind was still churning! Something over-the-top was what I needed.

Then my big break came! Yes, it was the last quiver from my depleted ammo pouch, but it held a lot of promise, I told myself. Pup had been locked in the barn, which he recognized as standard by now when my cousins came. Pup was a liability on these sojourns—he had proven that in the past! One whistle from either Mom or Dad or siblings even, and he felt obligated to respond by answering their call. The direction, Pup responded from was a dead-ringer give away where we guys were messing! This would then narrow our options when we heard someone call. Not having heard the call was tough to explain I found, when Pup had responded. But let's say we had not heard anyone calling without Pup there, that's a new ball game!

In the distance, over a half-mile away from our dugout, hiding inside a fair-sized wooded bluff of bush and tall trees sat the land baron's John Deere D tractor. Checking it out might be worthwhile and be classified as adventure. The big D was a clumsy, slow machine and so, rather than drive that steel critter back home to the land baron's yard several miles away, the hired men left the two-cylinder job hidden in the bush. What harm could be done by leaving the two tons of steel there over the weekend?

We wandered in the direction of the big engine but I did not announce my brewing plan at this point. My plan called for me to make a bold announcement that I would attempt to start the steel monster, knowing and hoping the critter would not fire up! In actual fact I had never driven this size of tractor before, but in "guy talk" I had driven Mr. Dan's big D, "a fair bit!"

We did a slow-pace walk about the machine, with some more guy talk. In our small talk, it was the opinion of my cousins that this beast was a real brute to start and would take a lot of experience to do so. My juices were flowing! With all the bravado I could muster, I announced with some gusto, "I will start the big D!" A side glance to my cousins, I saw them look at each other with dropped jaws!

I turned a few taps to see if the fuel would run as it ought to and it did, as well displaying some knowledge about the distillate burner. I felt I was scoring points with the cousins, but not a real shocker as yet for my buds. Having seen how the big D tractor was started in the threshing season, this tractor looked identical, with the little gismos and taps as Mr. Dan's big D had been at the threshing machine a few years back. Having satisfied myself that I might be able to pull off this advanced feat, I made my bold move!

Silence from my cousins, this was top shelf stuff, I could tell by their still dropped chins, their pale faces! That kind of reaction is what a young man needs to get the adrenaline flowing properly!

Yes, my juices were flowing now! Just announcing that I would start the steel monster was all I really could hope for, in fact, if it should start, that would be more than what I felt I could handle! My cousins stood back and watched in a mixture of shock and admiration of my guts at this undertaking. Now they had taken me seriously, that I was going to really start the big D!

Recalling that the distillate had to be drained and gas allowed to run into the ignition chamber, I proceeded as confidently as I could recall the moves Mr. Dan had made at the threshing machine, now many years ago. A veteran of 6 years or so was I with the big D! My recollection of the procedures was a mite rusty I found. At the same time, it was important to keep that cool "I know what I am doing" look in front of my cousins. The taps were turned, the levers all set as correctly as I knew how. It was time to make contact and fire up the big D, as proffered minutes ago! I ran my fingers through my hair, as grown-ups do when they want to show that deep thoughts are flowing through that productive brain!

I decided to do a walk about the tractor, a double check if you will; as well, I needed to talk to my inner self—it seemed as though two voices were talking at the same time! From the garbled voices, it seemed one was saying, "Call off this dumb idea," while the louder one was saying, "Go for it!" "It's always darkest just before dawn," Mom always said; it was dawn for me right now!

As I stood beside that flywheel on the big D, yes I had grown upwards! Now, I was about as high as the flywheel, still a few feet to the top of the jolly green giant.

"Stand clear," I offered; if you are going to pull a rogue, do it well! I was not short in the fake department, I told myself. I reversed the flywheel till I heard the big D inhale a huge breath, which was how Mr. Dan started his machine.

I gave the large flywheel a hefty spin and to my amazement (frankly disappointment, but hopefully not showing it), the big D let out a huge plume of smoke and began his huff, puff routine as per text book! This was a bittersweet moment for me! This was not supposed to happen! I was to swing the flywheel again and again, finally giving up in exhaustion! Now to keep cool was not easy! I did not for a moment think that the old tractor would fire up with the memory settings I used, and on the first spin! Oh for Mr. Dan to be able to see me now!

We were far from our house, but on a Sunday afternoon when everything is quiet in the serene, flat countryside, a big D huffing and puffing did cause my bravado to quiver as the noise did reverberate through the sunshine-filled, quiet prairie.

Doing another walk about the hissing machine, but more so being able to survey our farm from this angle behind the trembling tractor without appearing concerned. My cousins stood in awe of me! Our farm was over a half-mile away, could Dad or my siblings hear the tractor?

This was no time to turn sissy and shut the big D down, I re-assured myself. I took another look at my cousins—they were impressed, their faces showed it!. I wanted over-the-top action and I was now over-the-top with adventure!

Grouping my thoughts to the important here-and-now, I turned the gas tap off, switching the tractor to distillate fuel, I had nothing to lose since I was up to my eyeballs in trouble if spotted. In Dad's books, I knew I had crossed the line not by a wide margin, but over! With that last year's school debacle still likely stored in his mind, even a slight crossing of the line could cause in a closer tab being kept on future cousin visits.

The big D took the distillate without a sputter and was ready for action. The question now was, am I ready to take on the next challenge? These challenges were coming at me a bit faster than I had banked on! Another batch of adrenaline arrived just in time to ask the clincher question. At my, "Who is driving?" question, my cousins cowered; I was clearly "the man"!

At my invitation, my cousins hopped on the back deck of the vibrating steel monster with me. I threw the tractor into third gear and pushed the long lever forward.

Talk about the feeling an astronaut has when he hears the words "lift off"! That was my adrenaline surging through my blood vessels! The tractor obeyed my command and moved forward. Now, I had never actually driven a big D before, despite my claims to the otherwise! The steel steering wheel that Mr. Dan just spun around without seemingly an effort proved to be as much as I could handle or a bit more. Not being able to turn the steering wheel fast enough, I ran over some smaller trees but assured my cousins that everything was going as planned. I was at the wheel of several tons of power, with my ego barely missing the overhanging branches! Mr. Dan, where are you when I need you?

Staying in the small bush, which acted as my camouflage from our farm, was my silent goal. Therefore I ran over fallen tree logs, crunching them up with the huge steel cleats on the monsters rear wheels. Some barely missed larger trees did cause the perspiration under my arms to make me feel grown-up!

Judging from my cousins' expressions, I had scored all the points with them that were available as I continued to spin the steering wheel, I was getting the hang of it! Huge plumes of smoke bellowed out the top exhaust, the smoke seemed to know it was its last chance to make an impression today, as I pulled back on the wide open throttle! I steered the huge steel brute back to its original spot, pulling the long stop lever back, calling it a day! I weaned the motor of fuel, soon the tractors firing chamber was empty, with the machine coming to its last huff!

I glanced around to see if any problems might be showing on the horizon, namely our farmyard. There were none that I could spot, my bravado again replenished! Another mock machine walk about, but actually it was my way of checking back at our farm again!

The quiet Sunday afternoon carries sounds a long distance, I feared. Looking at someone's stationary machine, I knew was fine. But to have started the machine, driven it, even Dad would not attempt that! Why did that bugger machine have to fire up I thought for just for a split second! Then the sweet thought of the looks on my cousin's faces! Way over the top! Never could they match this!

I had scored mega-points with my cousins, with no price to pay! We had gone undetected! Dad and Unc's walk about on the farmyard yet some time away, I surmised. During such a walk about on the yard, Dad's attention would have been drawn to the noise. We were ahead of the folks, what a place to be!

The school lab experiments we guys had done about a year ago had come to Dad's attention, likely by the grumpy teacher who had no feel for young people doing homework on the weekend! The teacher. having detected some evidence of a fire, when the Bunsen burner had been out of fuel, he had explained to Dad. But since no "real damage" was the teacher able to claim, Dad, himself a bit of a rebel from the past, asked me to cool my heels a little; that chapter closed. Closed yes, but with parents, most anything from the past can be reopened if it helps their case today. Such advantages, again, kids did not have!

On our walk back towards home from this over-the-top tractor ride, I detoured my visitors through the Bergen's backyard. My confidence, or lack of it, said to approach our farmyard from a different angle, not to even raise suspicion should any exist, that our bods had been in the area of any bush noise that might have filtered through. The neighbour's bull was lying down, no threat to us as we tripped through the pasture. I always tried to stay clear of private buildings.

I laid the ground rules on each visit: no smashing, no damage of any kind; these rules were respected. The size of the garden, the number of birds, plus the tameness of the birds awed my guests as well. The always present slingshots in our back pockets were removed and the rubber stretched a few times. We dazed a few blackbirds, considering that a total mission completed.

Returning to our farmstead, with a leisure stroll look, taking up slingshot practice on some spare bottles in the backyard. Soon it was time for *faspa*, which we heartily partook of and it was time to say goodbye. What an afternoon! What an act to follow for my cousins when I would return the visit!

Just a few of the Zacharias'—rocky mountain clan—dropped in at grandparents for faspa"

Unc's Auto

When you are around the fourteen-year-old mark, stuck on a farm in Flatfields, your hand-me-down bicycle is on the fritz for the umpteenth time this year, a Sunday afternoon is not a pretty prospect. Your parents have gone into a combo of hibernation and middle age, stay at home snooze mode.

Farmyards, for the most part on a Sunday afternoon, are as silent as a morgue and any noise would be considered a disturbance by the sleeping folks. I had been well-warned to cool it! All that was left for me to do that was noiseless was sit and pout! The sun was beating down, a two-mile walk to a friend's house was not appealing to me. Sitting on an upside-down water pail, I was either moping, grouchy; perhaps down right mad covers it!

The dumb bike we had, had been a used piece of crap when we bought it. Then three older siblings had taken any life out of it that it may have had, and now it's my turn to have the dilapidated two wheels of wild transportation! This bike, whenever I did attempt a three mile trip, would give way about halfway, and I walked the dumb piece of steel back to the farm more often than I rode it home. The sprockets were all wore down and the chain slid off at will. The bent frame allowed a nut to slip on the rear fork, and the back wheel now rubbed on the fork, making riding impossible. Bleakly, I contemplated the boring afternoon ahead, which would be followed by sitting beside a sweaty cow that I would be attempting to milk or take revenge on.

A car on the main road in the distance caught my momentary attention. Anything that moved caught my attention, more than I could say for my life! The car slowed down, turning into our long driveway. Anything was an improvement over the present. The car came to a stop and my Uncle Abe and Aunt Helen from a distant town stepped out. Both of these people were the happy-go-lucky types. With a big grin, Uncle asks if the parents are at home. "Sure they are," I said. With those words I was in the house, knocking on the parents bedroom door. This I liked! Turns out Uncle and Auntie are on their way to a wedding that my parents were invited to, but decided to forgo in favour of a lazy sleep instead.

Uncle was a mechanic and drove the old "boxy" type of car, while most had the sleek lines of the forties. Unc kept his car in good shape, especially the mechanical part. Now my folks had been egged into joining them by our now guests for the wedding event in yonder village and Dad took our sleeker model car from the garage. Uncle, I am sure, saw the sultry mood I was celebrating. They were from a busy town, and here these fourteen-year-old hormones are cooped up on a boring farm in the middle of nowhere. Look up boring in the dictionary and you will see a picture of Flatfields! If you wanted any action you had to create it yourself. Rip Van Winkle was exciting compared to Flatfields!

As my parents and Uncle and Auntie were settling into our car, Uncle Abe looked at me and said "The keys are in the car and the tank is full," referring to his older boxy job, sitting idle on our yard. I had one of the best mood swings I can recall! Flatfields was boring no more!

Assessing my good fortune and waiting for our car to disappear down the road, I was ready for action! Collie Pup had checked out the wooden wheels on Unc's car. Pup preferred the wooden wheels, as he could wet one and by the time he did the last wheel the first one seemed ready for a second coat. Pup only quit after either his tank dried up or his hind leg gave out from lifting it to often!

My plans were clicking, rifle on back seat, a good supply of ammo, the car roared at my command. The stick shift was standard fare for me and I lost no time as I sped down our driveway on the way to my friend's house, some two miles away. My friend, too, was suffering from boredom till I showed up. He seemed to agree that my presence would turn boredom into excitement. I concede that I liked action, and, in Flatfields, you were on your own in that department.

A few words on my plans and he to agreed to get his rifle, although, for whatever reason, when he walked to the car my friend Barney walked with a stiff leg, as though he was "Hoss" on *Gunsmoke*. He had stuffed the gun barrel into his pant leg and the rest of the gun was under his loose shirt. His folks did not approve of any guns but he prevailed, having a gun with some restrictions. Sunday was one of the restrictions, which I was under as well at our house—a Mennonite thing!

We toured the countryside a bit, sassing a few friends that we had a car to ride in. Then came the country roads—I mean real country cow trails! This was Hutterite country and few, if any, roads were required for them and not desired by the Hutterites either. Wide implements were much easier to transport on cow trails than higher, narrower, maintained roads. The municipality did not mind less money to spend and yet collect full Hutterite taxes on the land.

On these country roads, the gophers were plentiful. Hutterites do not own guns, at least at that time.

Gophers, therefore, had little to fear and were rather interested. it seemed, that an enclosed vehicle would come down this road. Hutterites own only trucks, half-ton and large grain trucks. That has changed as vehicles changed and today Hutterite women can be seen barreling down the dusty roads in a suburban multi-seat van. In my day it was trucks only and women did not drive any vehicles.

Hutterites however did not mind—in fact, liked to see us hunt the all too plentiful gophers that were eating their grains. My friend and I "culled the flock" fairly well that afternoon. In fact, it was only when the ammo expired that we called it a day.

We drove back to our friend's house, drank some lemonade, recalling the events of the exciting afternoon. I wanted to be sure I had Uncle's car back and cooled down before they arrived back from the wedding feast. Cooling the car down would display some good judgement on my part, I reasoned.

Mennonite weddings were huge events. Invitations flowed freely, verbal and written. Family roots were discovered, recovered, at the festive meals. Homemade buns, coffee by the gallons, cheese, homemade sausage, homemade cookies rounded off the feast. The focus often was not the quality but the quantity of food. The women seemed to enjoy the preparing and serving of food, chattering throughout. The men sat in groups of ten or so but the make up of the group was changing constantly, as the men moved about to meet and greet as many other men as possible, giving them maximum info. Mennonites are a curious lot, I am proof of that as well! The kids were plentiful, but they kept busy playing with each other. Yes the bride and groom were there, but for the most part, visiting was the focus of going to a wedding. The wedding was the cause of the gathering but visiting was the event.

My uncle's car was safely at our yard and cooled down when the folks returned. In fact, I was now busy—cheerfully even—doing the chores only hours earlier I had dreaded. Thanks Unc!

Sneezin' Season

*n*ever a favourite activity of mine, but it had to be done—in my case, endured. That was the haying season for me. Hay was pitched by fork in my early days and my duty was on the hayrack, "loading the rack" as it was called.

But first let's cut the grass. This, for the most part, was Dad's job and involved two horses pulling the mowing machine. Half a mile of our property bordered a built up road, the grade was somewhat on a slope and sitting on the steel, shallow mower seat and guiding some ambitious horses could be trying. The mower scat was a perforated steel, rather shallow job, where sliding out of when on a slope was easier than staying put!

After the three-foot tall hay (at what point does grass turn into hay?) had been cut and had dried for several days, it was raking time. The raking involved me as a young lad. The horses also somewhat frustrated by the road grade were a bit harder to handle, and the racking machine seat was a carbon copy of the mower seat, steel, shallow and slippery—especially at an angle. The rack picked up the now-hay as it had been cut and gathered into large fluffy piles to pitch onto the hayrack, with hand and pitchfork.

Now the hay in piles, it was time for the loading of the hay and hauling the fodder to the hayloft. To get this precious winter fodder into the dry barn loft, an interesting sling was used to hoist it into the huge end door of the barn loft.

A sling was placed on half the hayrack floor, looking somewhat like a kite shape. It was ropes and wood slats, the width of the hayrack, about eight feet. One sling covered half the length of the rack, about eight feet as well. The other half came from the other end of the rack, meeting where a metal clasp held the two together. There was a long, light rope attached to the clasp, for release later in the loft.

The hay was now pitched onto the rack, and my duty was to spread the hay with a pitchfork so as to make an even load on the hayrack. Often we would have both Dad and Big Bro pitching the hay up onto the rack and Chubby with a pitchfork taller than me, trying to keep up the spreading job! Big Bro just loved to be on my case about me not working hard enough and keeping up with the spreading of the fodder. He felt my job was an easy touch compared to his pitching of hay down below. Again, as he enjoyed doing, forgot our seven year age difference! At that point I was about half his age!

Acrimonious occurrences were some, actually many, and since Dad needed both Big Bro and me for the haying season, so his was the role of peacekeeper! I do recall an instance or two where I had enough guff from Bro, went to the front of the rack and sat down in defiance. A mini version of the Boston Tea party I guess you could call it. Dad then came up with me on the rack and smoothed the problem over by helping me for a while and then returned to again help pitch the hay up to me, but at a more moderate pace. Bro was told to keep his peace and also be more moderate with his hay pitching. Older brothers are there to make life miserable for younger brothers I am told; Bro excelled!

Once the rack was half filled, another set of slings was laid on the hay, just like the first. The ritual of pitching and spreading the hay was repeated. The loaded rack was hauled to the end of the barn by our two trusty horses, Jack and Frank.

That pointy part of the barn roof you have seen many times, protruding some 12 feet past the end of the barn, comes into play. An iron rail runs the length of the barn loft, attached to the inside of the ceiling, to the end of the peak extension.

A very thick rope, about 2 inches in diameter, also follows the rail through a series of pulleys at the south end of the loft, back out the side loft window of the barn. The rope goes down and under another pulley that is attached to some poles, well anchored in the ground.

Here, the horses, now unhitched from the hayrack, are hitched to a whippletree that is attached to the horses' harness and the sturdy rope.

Let's review in reverse order. Horses are hitched to the rope that feeds through a pulley attached to poles on the ground level. Rope flows up through a small loft window. Through a pulley there and follow the rope to the south end of the barn (Hayrack is parked at the north end). Rope follows the heavy steel rail, attached to the barn peak, to the north end. Rope and heavy *gismel,* which defies description, now drop down unto the hayrack.

Let me try to make *"gismel"* a bit clearer. I feel this sling and lift contraption was very unique and perhaps even well ahead of its time, comparing this to other methods used in farming in that era. Imagine if you will, a bunch of grapes, the stem sticking straight up, using an electrical term, call it a male. Now think of fifty pounds. of steel (grapes) with some pulleys and rope running through it. The horses pulling the rope now pull "the bunch of grapes" with the stem heading for an opening at the top of the rail, the female, that is on wheels. Once this stem (male) pokes into the opening, triggers a release and the wheels take the entire "bunch of grapes" together with the sling of hay and it rides along the loft rail to the far end of the barn loft. Horses are stopped, the long dangling rope on the middle clasp now gets a tug from the loft operator, the clasp releases and you have a ton or more of dry hay explode in the loft.

Now, the barn loft is wide and would not hold as much hay if always dumped in the middle of the loft. Enter the smart loft operator, who, once the sling is hanging in the loft waiting to be dumped, but the operator now begins to push and pull the loaded sling, causing a swinging action. He aims the loaded sling for the far corner area and released the clasp at the joining bottom of the sling, at just the right point. The hay just flings to the empty corner, thus the entire loft will be filled. On the reverse, the empty slings now swing in the air as they ride the reverse trip, hit the end of the rail on the pointy part of the barn roof. The "grape stem" is now released and gently rides down as the horses are backing up. This of course is accomplished through a series of ropes and pulleys, which provide leverage.

Since our farm was the only one in the area to have this fine system, very unique and likely costly to install, I feel it's worth understanding such a work of art or technology of the 1900's and yet advanced beyond much of the other farm practices. A difficult system to describe, but a very versatile way of handling a lot of hay in the loft with a minimum of labour present.

The above holds true when all things are ideal, but when are they all on even keel? So on this one sling, Chubby had not been able to keep up on the spreading of the hay when filling the rack. This then resulted in an uneven load or sling of hay. Many times, with a wing and prayer, the sling would hold till at least in the barn loft before sliding sideways and out the grasp of the sling. The hay not landing at the place of choice but it was in the loft. There also were times when the lopsided load slipped out of the sling when it had reached the top of the barn peak then the gimel hooked into the long roof rail for the ride to the farthest point of the loft.

On occasion when the *gismel* hit the top entry point, a bit of a swing happened before the ride began. The flimsy sling load than chose to dump back unto the hayrack below. This unexpected release of the load just when the horses were leaning into their harnesses caused the pulling horses to leap forward and be startled. As you can imagine, there was no shortage of blame for such a mishap. It was at this point that I called a time out and was not on the rack for the next load. Dad did the spreading of the hay on the rack and by the time Dad and Bro came in with a load, peace had been restored and my haying continued! I had made my point and established my value, resulting in the respect the job deserved!

Even though the rope was two inches thick, they were known to break after years of wear and aging. Should that happen, the entire sling of hay would come crashing down back onto the hayrack. The horses would receive a sudden jolt when the rope broke, a bad scene! A new rope would have to be bought and was a major investment Dad had not budgeted for. But, we only bought one new rope in all my years of farming.

As you can imagine, the idea of hanging onto the side of the sling and riding up with the sling was my obsession. Always "Too dangerous" my dad said, till we had the new rope installed. Now it was safe, I argued. Dad relented and I was soon clinging to the sling ropes that held the hay in place. I clung to the loaded hay sling like a person repelling on a cliff side, my legs flaying about. The horses received the go signal and I was hanging unto the sling with all my might. About halfway up, had I been able to, I might have changed my mind. That was too late, I rode to the top and into the loft. I was safely removed before the powerful clasps on the sling were sprung, releasing the ton of fodder!

My dream had been lived! But the thought of me flaying about in the bright sunshine with my eyes foolishly looking to the ground did put the shivers in me, not admitted at the time, of course! The fact that I did not request another ride on the sling spoke volumes about my feelings. Next load of hay, I was again spreading the hay on the rack but I guess my excitement of the hayloft ride caused me to lose my concentration and my hay spreading was not evenly done. When we pulled the sling up at the barn, the unbalanced load lurched to one side and all the hay spilled onto the rack. I pleased no one, including me.

Load after load of hay was brought to the loft for dry storage. In wintertime, the hay was pitched down through a hole in the hayloft floor and into the hay room below. From here, we distributed the hay as required to the cattle.

When I was eleven years old, I was expected to handle the two horses when raking the hay in the field. Our two black horses were so well-trained and took an interest in their work that guiding the horses was a minor effort. Jack and Frank knew the drill and did it. It may sound a touch strange to suggest that "horses took an interest in their work." Not strange once you have worked with horses that do take an interest and those that don't care. Very similar to human that do care and do not care about their work.

Well-trained, fed, and respected horses will attempt to please their master all day! They understand what job you want to achieve. They remain alert if your duties, and thus theirs, change only a small amount of rein work is required to share your plans with them.

When the horses are hungry then the homeward bound turn is easier for them to take than the trip away from the farmyard. I have said it before, and bears repeating: next to a dog, your horse will be your best animal friend! I have seen evidence of horse's desire to please at many a threshing machine. When the master had emptied the rack of sheaves at the threshing machine, the reins tied to the rack front. The master would drop his fork on the rack floor, jump off the rack, walk to the coffee, sandwich wagon. The horses with empty rack made a circle, returning to the master, having a coffee and stop to wait for him to hop on board the rack again. Then they would trot back to the field and stop at the waiting sheaves of grain for the master to load. The master never touched the reins, never spoke a word! These horses were prized, respected and spoken to in caring—if not loving—respectful words and manners. It has been said that some Mennonite guys spoke softer to their horses than they did to their wives! Ouch! The good masters would talk to their horses with terms such as "Easy girls, relax girls" or if they were boys, the boy words would be used. Horses respond well to being talked to.

A good, proud master would not walk past his team without a kind comment and pats on the rump or nose nuzzle. The voice of the master has a great calming effect on them. Horses were also always fed and watered before the master went for his dinner. I always admired a master that had such a relationship with his horses!

Harness sores did happen on the horses and the thoughtful master kept an eye out for any signs of stress on the horse's body. If a tender spot was located, some salve and padding were placed at that spot, with a readjustment of the equipment made. Sadly, I have also seen horses with severe harness burn, and the master was oblivious or did not care; they were just a "beast of burden" to him. Should another good horse master notice this, it was reported to the threshing gang master and he ordered the careless driver to make changes and take care of the wound on his horse. Such a non-caring person was often at the barb end of stiff comments from good horse masters, as well as ignored in conversations, not considering his thoughts being worthwhile!

These poor horsemen were frowned upon as though they were wife beaters.

Jack and Frank were excellent, always wanting to please the master. When the black pair had served their days on our farm and were shipped away because of old age, I dropped more than a few tears! Dad was in mourning for weeks, but it was an act of kindness to retire them.

The gas tractor had taken over as well, with more modern farm practices a must to keep pace with the changing world, working horses just did not fit into the picture. Yes, I recall the tractors that replaced our two horses, but not with any fondness or sweet memories like Jack and Frank provided all my youth!

The loss of our horses was partially offset by the hay baler, which came along. The grass was mowed and dried and then swept into long rolls of the fluffy, dried hay. The baler, pulled by the snorting gas tractor, pulled the baler behind it, that gobbled up the dry hay and bound it into oblong bales. These hundred-pound bales were than loaded by hand onto the hayrack, and stacked high in the back farmyard. From here, the bales were hauled into the barn as the cattle required them in wintertime.

The loading of hay bales all day gave a young lad like me some bulging arm muscles that were admired by many. My town pals noted these muscles on me, while I was shorter than many guys were, I was never required to prove my strength as some had to, in a fight with another fellow. I respected peace and my pals accorded me a wide berth in my Saturday night town sojourns.

Driver Wanted

Being a farm lad was hard work! However, it had benefits as well. Having driven our pony with its wagon at age six, team of horses by age eight, it was a natural to drive the farm tractor by age ten. Each experience prepared me for the ultimate prize, the family car or truck!

In the rush of a full-blown harvest, my help on the farm was vital. Driving the half-ton grain truck by age eleven was therefore a reality for me. First it was strictly on the large combined stubble fields, moving the truck to the loaded combine bin. Once loaded, the trip to the farm bins was a real grown-up treat! Being able to back the loaded grain truck to the grain auger bin was quite an accomplishment.

Having performed rather well with the driving tasks entrusted to me, it came as little surprise that Dad allowed more responsible driving duties to come my way. Next spring Dad was enticed with a new crop—sugar beets. A very labour intensive crop it was. Long rows of tiny beets had to be hand-hoed and culled. Spacing and culling the tiny plants so as to give each plant room to expand as it grows without touching the next plant was a time-consuming and back-breaking chore.

Young neighbour's kids, eager to earn some bucks, were hired to help with the beet-hoeing job.

So at the age of twelve, Dad asked me to drive the Chevy

half-ton with a stick shift, around the neighbourhood and collect the kids that wanted to help with the hoeing. This had to be fun! I sat on the edge of the truck seat, which helped two ways—I could reach the brake and gas pedal, but equally important, I was able to look over the steering wheel making me feel grown-up! Each night I would again deliver them back to their homes. Despite my daredevil attitude at given times, driving was not one of them. The pleasure of driving was too great to risk messing up and be grounded! Sure, at times I was "egged on" to go faster or "get me home now"! But I was aware that one report to Dad that I had been reckless or irresponsible in my driving and I would likely have to wait four long years before my legal driver's license could be obtained. That's not say I did not ever "gun the truck" and make dirt fly, but I did so on a lonely country road with not a witness in sight!

I was also aware that some of my passenger guys were several years older than I was and their dads did not allow them to drive. A ting of jealousy was evident! If they could get me grounded by peer pressure to "gun the truck" or "make the dirt fly" they would be the first ones to rat on me, I suspected. I kept my cool and soon I was driving about the countryside with confidence. The RCMP were many miles away, very rarely drove the dusty country roads. In fact, the RCMP were several towns away and I do not recall ever seeing an RCMP car in the Flatfields area. Had I raised some trouble with my driving, it might have been reported.

Dad was turning more to specialty crops such as beets and sweet corn. We were the first farmers to grow sweet corn in the area and this called for more truck driving for me. Loads of sweet corn that had just been picked by hand was now hauled some fifteen miles to the cannery for processing. Taking the backcountry roads, I was able to sneak loads of corn to the cannery, unload and be back for another load without any problems! At times some waiting was required at the cannery to unload and some "shut eye" was possible, since the hours were 5 a.m. to 11 p.m. at night until the cornfields were picked, save Sundays. Some chicanery was also part of this waiting time to unload the cash product. In the small cafe at the cannery called a canteen, a young lad was shooting off his mouth as to his love of chocolate milk. On his dare that he could drink fifteen half- pints of chocolate milk, non stop, a group of men put their money on the table for the milk (some of my money as well). The young man somewhat slowly now laid his cash down, with the waitress to pick up the money, which pile of coins she would accept depended on the outcome of the heavy-drinking lad. If he drinks fifteen half-pints the waitress takes our money, if he fails, she takes his.

The cartons were lined up and opened as he drank. On the thirteenth carton the chocolate milk no longer disappeared, but the young lad did. The waitress scooped up his money and we re-divided our spoils, having had a good laugh. Somewhat wiser when he reappeared next day, with no mention made of his drinking prowess.

Jack Felde was "Village" police, night watchman and peacekeeper all rolled into one job. He was there when I first learned of the word Police. Mr. Felde was a kind man, a smile for everyone, the fatherly wave! Mr. Felde was also a very rotund man who enjoyed a donut or two, that reputation still is in effect for cops today!

Heard about the guy that tried his first holdup? He said—as he nervously tried his quick money escapade, that forty cops hit him before he got to the exit door. He agreed that a donut shop had been a poor choice to ply his new, short wayward career!

For many years Mr. Felde walked his beat. His uniform always neatly pressed, with the double-breasted coat (wrapped) tightly buttoned over his ample girth! The village tower bell was rung at store closing time each day. On Saturday nights, the tired store clerks listened for the bell to clang, meaning the twelve-hour shift was finished for them. Mr. Felde seemed to have no set hours of duty, he was a twenty-four hour type of Cop, night watchman, and bell-ringer as well, he also kept an eye for soft spots on the gravel streets. Plugged culverts fell into his duty to report to the street crew, consisting of one! As for physical labour, no one knew for sure if he was good at it, no one had seen him do any! Mr. Felde is the only guy I know that could talk more languages in one sentence than our former P.M. Chretien. He spoke some English, some High German and some Low German or *Platt Duetch*. The fact that he could throw all three languages at you in one sentence meant you had to have your bilingual ear on alert at all times!

A simple "Good Morning, how are you?" you could expect, *"guet"* (good) *"sieha fiine"* (very good) or just *"fine."* An upbeat comment about the events of the day or past few days, he was known to have a time lag, news wise. His somewhat blood shot eyes always puzzled me. Were these eyes for real or had he imbibed last night? Mr. Felde, whatever his native tongue, fit into the ninety-nine percent Mennonite community. I know not of an enemy he had!

Rare as car accidents were in those days, two cars had collided and Mr. Felde presided. Even though it was but a fender-bender accident, Mr. Felde treated it like a crime scene! Getting the full details from each accident party was a must! After his in-depth interview or report from the first party, he concluded with *"Du bist rictch"* (you are right). Now the seconds victim's turn, pages of notes, which concluded with *"Du bist auch richtig"* (you are also right). Mr. Felde made no enemies!

Later in his days, as the village became a town, now as town policeman, Mr.Felde bought a car, a 1939 Ford Coupe to be exact! Black of course (all cop cars were black back then) but always shiny clean. He felt he had an image to present and uphold as an officer of the law and he did that! The car now allowed him the pursuit option, overlooking the fact that the driver was still the same man!

A car later in life meant he learned to drive later in life. While Mr. Felde was dead serious about his work and did a great job, a comedy it was at times!

Try this picture, '39 Ford coupe, seat way back to accommodate his ample midriff behind the steering wheel. Seat lean also back, but his feet did require to give direction to the pedals! The only option to accommodate both midriff and pedals, slide down low! His large, old-fashioned Police cap, barely over the height of the steering wheel. Head turning from side to side as he rode down the street searching for any misdeeds. Most cases ended up with a warning to the offender, once the driver explained the special circumstances that caused him to be traveling twice the speed limit or had missed a stop sign! The Mayor, Councillors and wives were not subject to his scrutiny! Nor were the affluent businessmen! The poor farmer that came to Town so rarely, well he gave them a break too! Mr. Felde ruled with love, not law! Yet, when on rare occasion his dander did show up, he was a mean dude! Ask any drunk that he hustled into the one tiny cell the town jail held.

On Saturday night, the town marching band wanted a workout. Mr. Felde allowed the marching band to strut, shut down the main street of Winkler on minute's notice! Great sound they were too! Shoppers and merchants might have had a few delays or missed business as they marched, but the enjoyment the band gave everyone outweighed any inconvenience!

Father time was moving on while Mr. Felde's was standing still or so he thought. It was now in the mid to later 1950s. Cars now had horsepower, Mr. Felde still had his 1939 Ford with a lawnmower-sized engine. When he saw a young buck speeding in his power wheels, Mr. Felde felt duty-bound to pursue the culprits. As the speeding car left a cloud of dust behind, Mr. Felde jumped his car, into gear he booted the willing wheels. His head leaned back even a bit more as the G forces of this "dune buggy engine" kicked in, whatever the engine produced or he imagined it might produce! Several miles behind his prey by now, he bravely motored on. At times the guys in the power cars would turn around and meet Mr.Felde on their return trip, with Mr. Felde still in pursuit in the opposite direction. Again the lad-laden power car would turn around and now pass Mr. Felde at breakneck speed, disappearing down a dusty side road, which Mr. Felde choose not to follow. Should he have recognized the young man making a mockery of the law, he would talk to the father of the young driver at a later date. This was rather effective, as most of these young bucks were living at home and backing up to Dad's overhead gas tank to fill up. This did give Dad some clout! The sight was "Al Capone-style" all over again! Mr. Felde's favorite expression was *"dummer kiddle,"* (dumb fellow) when he spotted an infraction taking place.

The Town Fathers with mercy and wisdom gave Police Felde a well-deserved retirement package and hired a younger gun with a more competitive car and competence to deal with the changing world of policing.

Another interesting "Town Father" was Mr. Jackman. I call him a town father, but he really was a retired farmer, businessman type. Mr. Jackman knew all the fathers in the area and was an alert type of guy. How he was made, or given the title of "Justice of the Peace" is unknown to most memories. Mr. Jackman, much like Mr. Felde, worked on the principle that every human being makes mistakes and ought to be given a second chance. If however a young lad (girls did not get into legal problems in those days) did not get the message after being talked to the first time, Mr. Jackman could be tough as well. Going to see Mr. Jackman was the toughest thing to do. I did have to see him one time and I no longer remember why, honestly! I do remember walking to the front door of his home, (he worked out of his house) and Mrs. Jackman, with a wide smile, asked if I could come back a bit later allowing Mr. Jackman to finish his supper. Great Gads, I thought! Mr. Jackman on a full stomach will enjoy cutting up a young buck like me! I was right, in his kindly ways, he asked me to describe what had happened, who my father was. Seems to me that it was a missed stop sign he was addressing. Over an hour, with a few belches in between, he helped me "understand the rules of the road"! He was in the 80-year old range, the two dollar fine became nebulous, just let me go!

Had he torn a strip off me, it would have been much easier, but instead he said he understood me and why my driving infraction happened. Mr. Jackman said he had seen many a young lad break into tears as he was helping identify where the lad had gone wrong. He helped many a young man to get onto the straight narrow way and to have him remain there. Mr. Jackman was a good storyteller and would take the time to visit with a lad after the infraction had been adequately dealt with. For the life of me I cannot remember any of his stories but do remember they were interesting and even if marginally so, you did pay attention, his friendly face demanded it!

A few days later I happened to catch up with the aging Mr. Jackman as he was motoring down the street in town. While his speed was below the required, he ran not one but two stop signs that I witnessed!

Dad just smiled as I was attempting to make a point, dang those adults!

Planting the Mennonite staple, potatos!

Rural Rink Rats

A fine crop of young, male, hormone-surging bodies Flatfields had in my day! Hockey was just coming into its own on the prairies! Some towns like Winkler and Plum Coulee had open-air hockey rinks. Winkler, being the larger population, was in the process of building an enclosed hockey rink.

I recall, as a lad of about ten years old, when a carload of Flatfielders ran into town to watch our first enclosed rink hockey game. It was exciting! Who the gallant combatants were slips my mind, but no doubt Winkler Royals will have been the half of them. Watching the hockey game being played, inspired us stubble jumpers to want build an ice rink, open air of course, on one of our farmyards.

Two items were a must, one a flat piece of land that could be flooded for ice purposes, and secondly a good supply of water to flood the field with, for the large sheet of ice. A third item, while not an absolute must, were the boards for the sides of the rink, so one had solid bounds to keep the puck in play.

The third item, the boards, proved frustrating and challenging! Today's world where young people are catered to and pampered is a far cry from the cooperation we received from "so-called leaders," at least, elected officials, back then!

If you had a new idea and the gall to verbalize such forward thinking, certainly you were up to no good! Sport was human energy wasted, energy that should have been invested in farm labour!

A neighbour family had agreed to allow a chunk of pasture to be flooded. The water supply was the dugout nearby. Planks were what was needed to be frozen in place, all around the proposed rink, to make the game playable.

I knew just the place to get the required planks, with a zero budget. A bridge had been rebuilt not that many miles away and the old planks were just lying there, further rotting in the ditch! These foot high, twelve foot long, three-inch thick planks would just rot away before being used by the Municipality. Sure the one side of the planks had been wore out in grooves and splinters but the backside was level and would serve hockey well.

In hindsight, we should have just gone down, loaded the planks, forget about those supposed adults who must have grown-up thinking that navel gazing was exciting! If only these elected fruitcakes could have stopped the earth's rotation, that would have called for a party! So many Mennonite elected leaders must have lived with sore heels most of their life from digging them in and holding back on anything they felt was moving forward or changing!

Being the model citizen type, we sought permission from the municipality, which in fact owned the useless planks—at least useless to them and anyone else, except for firewood.

The hierarchy in the area who we had elected Councillor, acted as "small gods" over an area of six miles by six miles (Area sizes varied). There were approximately six councillors and they answered to "the bigger elected czar," also known as the Reeve.

So in our endeavor to be good citizens, we made a request to the Councillor for the area for the use of the planks. Firstly he inquired where these planks were that we were referring to, since he was not aware of their existence. "Much too large a decision to make for him on his own," so he would have to talk to the Reeve about some stinken' old planks that were nothing more than firewood! Youth was really getting too rambunctious, was the facial read the Councillor left us with. Like, who do you think you are? The Toronto Maple Leafs? The Montreal Canadians? Things happen and are fine to hear about, providing they are far from our little protected "bubble zone" called Flatlands, filled with stuffy Mennonites!

We young men forgot that Mennonite boys are not supposed make things happen, we are to shake our heads and just watch things happen, "Like us adults do," he was saying with his eyes! More delays, more waiting, more red tape, the winter season was wearing on, which of course was precisely what this elected jughead was hoping for—spring comes, another problem solved!

My dad, who was not the most enthused guy about sports, knew he had an angry young son on his hands. Yes, Dad also saw that new ideas were not all bad, unlike so many stuffy thinkers of the day!

Dad did have some youthful spunk in him and would have loved to enjoy sports instead of having to tend an illegal liquor still on the back of the farm in Rocky Mountain country as he grew up.

My dad's father was killed at a young age in a rare train wreck. His mother remarried, then his mother passed away and the "step-parents" of life shaped much of his youth.

It was the prohibition era, times were tough—like desperation tough! Crops had failed and some cattle sold off for cash and feed conservation.

Booze was in demand and the farm Dad lived on was located but a scant few miles off the American border. The USA was where the booze market was strongest, homebrew! Stepdad saw a market he could tap making homebrew. The old straw stack that had been "threshed upon" for decades was the perfect camouflage for a homebrew still, and he was right! Threshed upon meant a new layer of straw was added each year, but the base of the stack became hard, almost petrified.

The huge straw stack was more cave than useful straw stack and in the hollows and burrows the cattle had created over the years was where the brewmaster set his illegal still, dead smack in the middle of the hardened stack. Listening to my dad alluding to his youth, one had to have a good memory. Dad would start a story and than clam up, a month, a year or longer, then he would add "another piece to the youthful puzzle" he was compelled to grow up in. Dad choked up! Some info, well, I had to complete as best I could on my own, which is what you are reading.

Needless to say, Stepdad required my dad to operate the still at night, if food, clothe, and warm room meant something to this young lad, my dad! The brewing of the illegal booze was done mostly at night. The brew was transported by horse and buggy across the Canada/USA border, which was unguarded at the time or if it was protected it was a hit and miss affair. The booze was in legitimate standard farm cream cans, the five-gallon type. Dad's stepfather was an accomplished smuggler, had a ready market, he knew where to turn the liquid booty into cash! My dad, in his dependency, had no choice but to work the still if you wanted to eat and sleep at this house.

The brew inspectors felt that this farm was producing illegal booze, but search after search, the inspectors came up empty-handed. All the barns and sheds were searched, but the inspectors came up dry, while the farm was "plenty wet"! Step dad made sure that the cattle and huge snorting bull were always roaming the straw stack area during the day when inspectors did their thing! This was where the loaded hayrack was parked for the cattle to feed off of. The inspectors never suspected a straw stack could house such an enterprise, as one can understand. Not prone to saunter into a straw stack area that had a 2000 pound bull looking to trample something, the frustrated inspectors left scratching their heads!

How long this trade carried on is a guess to me, but my dad when he was a bit older, put his foot down with stepdad and said "That's it!" Stepdad had little choice but to shut the cash machine down. Should my dad decide to "talk," stepdad would have gotten free room and board in the Crowbar Inn!

The illegal still must have been operating for a number of years, since Dad at first, due to age, had no choice to comply by working the still at night. But as Dad grew up, they had "heated words" about the still, and finally Dad drew a line in the soil and asked stepdad to take the step across the old western dispute line! Stepdad dared not and Dad no longer was a brewmaster!

So Dad was pleased to raise his kids in such a positive environment as Flatfields! Dad also wanted to allow his kids to enjoy freedoms denied him. The question was, how much rope do you allow the kids for their own good? Secondly he had to think of the church and its yesterday's leadership.

Sometime after we received the cold shoulder from the Councillor of the area about the planks we needed for the ice rink, the Reeve, who was a friend of Dad's, happened onto our yard for a friendly chat. The fact that Council and Reeve elections were in the air may have prompted the visit a touch as well.

The question of the use of planks was asked and the OK was given without a further thought.

The ice rink was built and provided endless hours of hockey and open nights for all of Flatfields to enjoy pleasure skating.

More Books to Come

The first book was only to lay the "ground work" for more editions. In each following book (the Lord willing) I will again "grow up" beginning with my youngest memories. Some chapters will contain the following: The adventures of my great aunts, driving a Model T. coupe, which my Dad serviced and took for trial runs—never without me at his side. The roan ranger horse that our family had a love-hate relationship with—but the horse won

the day. Oh yes, every young man must try some smokes—in my case, it was a cigar—my tummy has never been the same. My ongoing battle with my older bro. He caused me to become a man—overnight. Winkler's Jewish joint—as it was known at the time. An entire day with Max Gladstone. Jack rabbits filled with water to add weight? Mennonite porkers—pig killing bees were the highlight of the season. The topless tin Lizzie—what a wedding that was! Remember the electric fence? A dog and cat on our farm do. The villages! What a story they were—maybe are today—read the ratings… the "F" word comes up in this story—the Friesens and Froeses. Many more state-of-the-art stories of the past as I remember them.

ORDER FORM

To order additional copies of *Rappelling the Mennonite Mountain*, please use the order form below or contact the author directly.

ORDERED BY: (PLEASE PRINT)

Name: _____

Address: _____

City: _____ Prov./State: _____

Postal/Zip Code:_____ Tel.: _____

_____Copies @ $19.95: $_____

Shipping ($4.00 1st book - $1.00 each add.): $_____

G.S.T. @ 7% *(Canadian residents only)*: $_____

   Total: $_____

PAYABLE BY:

❑ Cheque   ❑ Money Order   ❑ VISA   ❑ MasterCard

Credit Card #: _____Exp.:_____

Signature: _____

SEND TO: Essence Publishing, 20 Hanna Court
Belleville, Ontario, Canada K8P 5J2

**To order by phone, call our toll-free number,
1 (800) 238-6376, ext. 7575
and have your credit card handy.**

You can also order online at www.essencebookstore.com